D1579634

# A BISHOP AT PRAYER

# A BISHOP AT PRAYER

## Leslie E. Stradling

*Anglican Bishop
of Johannesburg*

LONDON

S·P·C·K

1971

*First published in 1971*
*by S.P.C.K.*
*Holy Trinity Church*
*Marylebone Road*
*London N.W. 1*

*Made and printed in Great Britain by*
*Willmer Brothers Limited, Birkenhead*

SBN 281 02603 3

# CONTENTS

# 1

## MODERN SPIRITUALITY

A white man was sitting on the pavement, his back propped up against a window of the bottle-store. His chin was gashed and bleeding, as from a fall, and he was obviously rather drunk. A young policeman was squatting beside him, quietly trying to find out how he could help him. About twenty men —multi-racial as all such Johannesburg crowds are—were looking on in fascination.

My first reaction was one of anger, and I am not sure how to analyse this. It was partly that a privileged white man should so demean himself before Africans, but I think it was specially anger that he was being treated with such sympathy. Had he had a black skin, he would by now have been bundled, without any sympathy at all, into a police-van.

As I walked away, I found myself asking God to forgive me for my anger, and thanking him for the compassion shown by the policeman because, although some other police methods are wrong, this one was right. I went on to ask God that he would make me always more anxious to praise what is right than to blame what is wrong. I don't mean that I drifted along the street in a holy haze, bumping into light standards and ignoring acquaintances, but rather that these thoughts arose in my mind at the time and were subsequently turned more clearly into devotions when I was next praying in church.

But why should I suppose that anyone will be interested in the things I pray about, or where and how I pray? I certainly do not consider myself to be an expert on the subject. The books on prayer are innumerable, and many of them are written by people who undoubtedly are experts. But most of the ones that I have read either discuss the theology of prayer, or give instruction on how we should pray, or offer advice about the problems encountered in prayer. It seemed to me that, if I could describe the way in which I, a beginner, actually pray, it might encourage those who pray in the same sort of way as I do, and also give some help to those for whom prayer is a puzzle or a muddle. The greatest satisfaction that I could gain from writing this book would be to know that I had stimulated someone to pray better in whatever way it was right for him to pray—and that might be in a very different way from mine.

---

> Brethren, at this synod eucharist we have come together as a diocese to praise God, to share in the benefits of his eternal sacrifice, to thank him for his mercies to us during the past year, to confess to him our corporate shortcomings, to pray for each other and for God's Church throughout the world, and to seek his guidance in our deliberations.

The congregation reacted with the blank stare that is reserved for pious platitudes, sank back as comfortably as it is possible to sink back into a church pew, and prepared themselves for boredom until such time as a controversial section of the charge was reached.

But in fact I was being highly controversial, for everything I said is questioned now. Agnostics and humanists have always questioned it, but in these days there are Christians who are equally critical. I am not thinking of the "God is dead" school, who have, I believe, done us good by forcing us to take a look at many of our suppositions. I refer to those writers who say that prayer in the traditional sense is no longer possible, because they do not believe in a "God out there" to whom they can pray. So before I can tell you how I try to pray, I must first attempt to justify the fact that I pray at all.

All my life, when I have been talking to God, I have regarded him as a person. But to leave it like that would be a false simplification. The basic Christian doctrine of the Holy Trinity tells us that God is not *a* person, but three persons in one God. Moreover when this doctrine was first formulated the word "person" had a vaguer meaning than it has now. Today we think of a person as a conscious centre of existence. He is someone who is self-contained. He is separated from other persons, however outgoing he may be, and however able to communicate with other persons. If we press the word person as applied to God, it seems to me that we shall not only end up with three Gods, but these three Gods will be separate from the world that between them they have made. God is there and the world is here and, just as the world is finite, so we have a finite God. But God who is finite is not God as the Christian understands him.

So I find it better to think of God as Being, and to say that Being is personal, though it is a great deal more than personal. God acts in a personal way through history, through the Church, through my own life. If this is symbolic language, it is the best symbol that we have, because personal being reveals God's creativity and love in a richer way than anything else on earth. The reason why I can say this is that, when God wanted to reveal to us the mystery of his being, he did so through a person—Jesus Christ.

And if it is true that Jesus is the great revelation of Being, then we can with confidence learn from him how we are to think of Being. Jesus always addressed God in a personal way. The word "Father" is characteristic of his teaching. You can, if you like, say that this is to speak in an anthropomorphic way, but that is the way Jesus spoke, and it is good enough for me. If I am going to pray in and through Jesus Christ, I must pray as he did.

Lord, I adore you in the mystery of your being. Nevertheless I adore *you* whom I can address as father. I adore *you* whom I can address as lord and saviour. I adore *you* whom I can address as sanctifier.

Lord, make me less sure that I know any of the answers

to the problems of deity, and make me more sure in you, my God.

If I did not believe that God is personal I do not see how I could pray. Because I have a living, personal faith—though I know that this is often fragile and always inadequate—I cannot help praying.

It becomes another thing, however, when God is identified with the universe; when it is said, as some radical theologians seem to say, that he *is* the stream of evolution. This is no new problem. Before Christ came, both pantheism and dualism were well-known theories, and Christian thinkers themselves have always wondered how God can be both transcendent and immanent, both "out there" and in our midst; how Jesus Christ can be at the same time both God and Man, how the infinite God can be also the saviour of men in finite space.

I was brought up to believe that these are real perplexities which must be honestly accepted. We cannot understand them, yet we know that these seeming contradictions are a part of reality. My limited mind cannot hope to explain them, but revelation, together with experience—the experience of the Church made real to me in my own experience—assures me that they are true. "As both transcendent and immanent, God is at once beyond every possible being and yet present and manifest in every one of these beings."[1]

But some modern theologians will have none of this. For them God is one with the world. God is not only Being, but everything that is is God.

The point that I want to make now is this. If that was what I believed, then prayer in the sense that I have always understood it would be impossible for me. If there is to be dialogue, there must in some sense be two persons talking and listening to each other. If there is no God beyond me, I cannot talk to him, nor can he answer me. The most that can happen is that, instead of picking up the telephone and talking to a "God out there", I can pick up the intercom and talk to someone in another room of the same office block.

[1] John Macquarrie, *Principles of Christian Theology*, p. 187.

In other words, the new spirituality, as this phrase is used in certain circles, claims that in prayer we are talking to ourselves and to one another. I may have misunderstood him, but this is the impression I gained from reading a book by Canon Douglas Rhymes of Southwark Cathedral called *Prayer in the Secular City*. Meditation is no more than reflecting upon our experience, pondering on the meaning of life. Prayer for others means serving others. Prayer for guidance is looking for it in the advice of others. Penitence is asking others for forgiveness. Any prayer beginning with the word "Lord" or its equivalent is out.

This view of God and of prayer satisfies many people today. They claim that it gets rid of the distinction between sacred and secular, and that it speaks to the existential mood of our time. It does not, however, satisfy me, because I and many others are still convinced that the scriptures remain the main source of revelation. In the bible I find a God who is other than man. God stands over against us. He speaks to us and asks us—orders us—to do what he wants. He judges us. He forgives us. He saves us. He loves us. I find that the God of the bible is closer to me than breathing, but he is also a God who is "out there". I certainly meet the eternal Thou in my experience of other people, and in the world of nature, but he is for me at the same time the Other, the Beyond.

Jesus says: "Lo, I am with you." He says: "Come to me." He says: "Ask and I will give you." He confronts the disciples during Eastertide. He confronts Paul at Damascus and Corinth. He confronts the seven churches of Asia Minor. The same thing is confirmed by the experience of Christian prayer down the ages. In prayer we are speaking and listening, not to a life force or to love as the ground of our being, but to a divine lover. The crisis about prayer is in fact a crisis about belief in God.

Lord, they say that we can no longer address you as You,
 because that would be to make you a person, one person
 among many persons.

Lord, in my young days we just said You, and perhaps we

did not think enough about the difficulties involved in doing so. At any rate we understood one thing—our insignificance as man; for it was this that made us look up to you. I desire to hang on at all costs to this insight, for otherwise I should have so exaggerated an idea of my own importance that your transcendence would be swallowed up by your immanence in us.

Lord, we think that we are it—and yet science itself warns us that this is not so. With the discoveries of Copernicus we lost our centrality in the universe. With the discoveries of Darwin we lost our uniqueness in creation. With the discoveries of Freud we lost the illusion that we were in control of ourselves.[1]

Lord, unless you are You, and can be so addressed, we have lost everything. But if you are there, though we have nothing, yet we have all.

When I come across radical theologians who are, as it seems to me, preaching something less than the Church's truth as I understand it, what am I to do about it? If I keep quiet and just get on with believing and praying in my own way, it looks as if I am forgetting my job, as a bishop, to "drive away all erroneous and strange doctrine contrary to God's Word". But I have never believed that we get very far by denouncing others, especially when they are sincere seekers after the truth. I am glad that these people at least believe in the immanence of God. It is possible that I can help them most by continuing to remain in close relationship with them, and by praying for them that the transcendent may one day break in upon them. Certainly I must respect their integrity and, as far as prayer is concerned, I encourage them to go on praying in any way that they can.

Now I am aware that this sounds terribly condescending. It suggests that I know more about God than—to name only one name among many—Bishop Robinson does. I fully realize in fact that I am not in the same class as he is, as far as

[1] I have forgotten the source of this quotation.

concerns expertise in theology and ability to communicate with the contemporary world. I have said what I have said only because I believe that God has revealed to me, babe as I am, something so deep and precious that I could not call it merely one opinion among others about God.

I want to go further and look at the positive truth that these writers are emphasizing, because I am sure that it is a truth which God is teaching us again through them. It is that we have too often divorced prayer and life. I used to be attracted by the statement that prayer is a turning away from the world, that it is a process of disengagement. I suppose I used to think—I cannot remember—that such withdrawal was wrong unless it prepared me for closer involvement in the world. This aspect is certainly more central to my thinking now, but there is more in it than that. I now believe that the statement is true only if we in some sense involve the world in our prayer. This takes us back to the teaching of Isaiah and other great prophets, with their denunciation of pious professions that are coupled with conduct which denies those professions.

It is not hard to observe this fault in others. Looking back we can see it, for example, in those many generations of Christians who prayed regularly every Sunday, but who kept slaves in their own households. (And we could find other examples nearer home.) From the point of view of our modern enlightenment, we could say that such people were hypocrites, but I myself find it easy to believe that they were pious and sincere, though their religion was incomplete and their turning to God only partial. I find it easy to believe this because I know that it is true in my own life. For part of the time I really do love and serve God. At other times, and in other parts of my life, I am so deaf to his commands that I do not even realize what it is that I ought to be doing for him. We cannot be satisfied until prayer, so far from being one of our many activities, controls every single part of our life.

The failure to understand this accounts for some of the current unease about prayer, even among those who still hold the orthodox Christian belief. Clergymen who have followed for years the methods of prayer taught to them in their theological colleges tell me that they now find these methods dry and empty. Lay people say that they don't know how to pray any more, and the prayer manuals which have been popular for so long appear to mean little today.

Some of this may well arise from the general uncertainty of the world in which we live, or from the inability to think of God as personal any more. But in other cases the root trouble is this separation of prayer from the experience of life. When this is so, we have to learn all over again how to pray, and I for one thank the critics for having stirred me up to do that.

So the phrase "the new spirituality" is used in two senses, and it is important to realize this, for sometimes the two seem to overlap or become confused. There is the new spirituality which is the expression of radical theology, which cannot conceive of God as other than immanent in this world, and which accordingly has devised a method of prayer that does away with all thoughts of transcendence. But there is also the new spirituality which, on the basis of traditional views about God, seeks to express its prayer life in ways more congenial to the present age.

It is about this second concept that the 1968 Lambeth Conference spoke to us. Resolution 4 says:

> The Church should search to discover those forms of spirituality and methods of prayer, both corporate and personal, which meet the needs of men and women today, such as those expressed by Abbé Michel Quoist in his book *Prayers of Life*. The Church should pay more attention to the development of that capacity for silent prayer which exists in all her members, and should encourage corporate and personal waiting upon God.

It is the new spirituality in this sense that I find relevant to my own prayers, and it is about this that I shall be writing in the rest of this book.

# 2

## THE NEW LOOK IN PRAYER

The first time that I used "modern" prayers in public was at a Three Hours service. Many people did not like them because they were too modern, and others appreciated them precisely because they were modern. I had first become interested in this type of prayer from paternalistic motives. Some of my (and there is no more paternalistic word than that) young people told me that they found such prayer helpful, and so I wanted to know what it was all about; much as I like to know a little about pop music, not because I enjoy it particularly, but because it is something that appeals to my teenage friends.

Having started in this superior fashion I soon found that there was a great deal that I could learn from it, and also that it was in essence the kind of prayer that I had always tried, however ineffectively, to use myself.

But first let us take a look at some of the people who are writing what has been called "pop prayer".[1] The book that is best known in South Africa, and the one which has been found to be most generally useful, is *Prayers of Life* by Michel Quoist. This was first published in 1954, but it was not translated into English until 1963. It is French in outlook and Roman Catholic, but on the whole the ideas come through easily enough to an Anglican. For example, in a short prayer called "The Telephone", the writer wonders why someone had rung up. He then realizes that, because he himself had done all the talking, he had failed to listen to what the caller had wanted to say. "Forgive me, Lord, for we were connected, and now we are cut off."

[1]For this section cf. John Robinson, *But that I can't believe*, chapter 23.

15

Michel Quoist did not invent this style of prayer. In his introduction he acknowledges his debt to Charles Péguy, that vigorous French catholic who lost his faith and then found it again. Readers of his *God Speaks* will recognize at once the source that inspired such a prayer as "I like youngsters"; and they will also know how far behind his master Quoist is when he writes about the Virgin Mary.[1]

In one sense there is nothing at all modern about this type of prayer, except that everything which I experience is, of course, modern for me. St Francis, Pierre Charles, de Caussade and others knew a good deal about it long before our era. One of my favourite Anglican classics is *Good Thoughts for Bad Times* by Thomas Fuller, written in 1645. Fuller was the rector of a parish in Dorset, and one of his prayers starts like this: "Lord, today I remembered my breakfast, but forgot my prayers." We can go back a good deal further, and find St Augustine writing the story of his life in the form of a prayer. He simply tells God in great detail what he has done and thought and said.

The writer of Proverbs (24.30ff.) is an even earlier example. He was walking past a farm one day, and he saw the vines choked by thorns and nettles and the stone wall broken down. I do not have to make many changes to turn his prayer into my own:

> Lord, I am often inclined to a little sleep, a little drowsiness, a little folding of the arms, so as to take life more easily. I call it little, but the sum total of many littles is big and, before I realize what is happening, spiritual poverty is at my elbow, and I have nothing to give.

> Lord, deliver me from temptations to sloth and, in all my prayers, grant me to see, look, consider well, and receive instruction (v. 32) from the life themes that you set before me.

A book of prayers which has had a wider sale than *Prayers of*

[1]Compare "Jesus meets his Mother" with Péguy's "Passion of our Lady".

*Life* is Malcolm Boyd's *Are you running with me, Jesus?* Many people have criticized this as being too American, too subjective, lacking in penitence, lacking in this, that, and the other aspect of the Christian faith. Such criticism misunderstands Malcolm Boyd's intention.

He was not writing prayers to be used in church. In public prayers I believe that there should be a certain timelessness and impersonality, so that all those who are present can join in. Perhaps I was wrong to use "pop prayers" in church on Good Friday, but I thought that this was an exceptional occasion, when people might be taught something about personal prayer.

Nor was Malcolm Boyd writing a book for others to use in their private devotions. I myself could not read a few pages from *Are you running with me, Jesus?* before breakfast, and then think that I had performed my religious duties for the day; but I do know that I have learned a good deal about how to pray from him. What we are doing when we read this book is to listen to Malcolm Boyd as he says his prayers. We know that he is an American, so it is absurd for us to criticize him for talking in the American idiom. I am glad that he trusts me enough to reveal himself to me as he is, and not as the book reviewers think that he ought to be. He prays about such matters as war and peace, films, problems of race and sex, and life on the campus.

In one of them, for instance, he speaks of the drinks that are tranquillizing him, helping him to take it, and then he remembers Jesus, who didn't go in for tranquillizers or put on an act, but who was always himself, living on a cutting edge; and he asks for help to do the same.

Carl Burke, in *Treat me cool, Lord,* brings us some prayers of delinquent teenagers whose honesty shines through their ungrammatical language. Less obtrusive, less shocking, more English, are the prayers of Monica Furlong.[1] In *Creative Brooding* Robert Raines takes an extract from a contemporary book or article or interview, links it with passages of scripture, and sums up the theme in a short prayer, such as: "Make me

[1] *Our Response to God:* July-August 1967.

17

care enough to commit myself and get involved." Norman Goodacre[1] speaks of the new theology which "makes him panic", and goes on to say: "Show me how I can begin to see the manysidedness of truth."

*That Man is You* by Louis Evely is not obviously a book of prayers at all, and yet I have found it a greater help to my own prayers than any of these others. It is a series of meditations in the classical tradition, but it is very much aware of the modern world. Thus in writing about a Retreat, and the need to get away from ourselves, he speaks of retreatants who bring with them books and unanswered letters and even a railway time-table in case they want to escape. "We all feel the need of a few projects to shield us from God." Instead of this we should disencumber ourselves of our problems and leave God to worry about them. It doesn't take much imagination to translate this into: "Lord, I feel the need of a few projects to shield myself from you."

In *Spirituality for Today*, edited by Eric James, many of the questions that I am trying to look at now, and many of the problems underlying them, are raised in a provocative way, the first chapter by John B. Coburn being particularly interesting. If it seems that the answers are not given with equal clarity, this probably means that they are different for each person who prays, and that no more than guide-lines can be suggested.

I could go on for pages giving illustrations from the books of those who are writing "modern prayers", but this is enough to give the general idea. When I myself try to pray in this manner, I find four main characteristics which distinguish it from the prayers on which I was brought up. I do not include among the four the fact that I am speaking as a person to a personal God—to a God who has shown himself to me in Jesus Christ and who is my neighbour—because this is something which has always been clear to me. Or at least, when I have doubted it, I have doubted also the possibility of prayer itself. Impersonal prayer has never been for me a live option.

First there is the question of language. To use "thee" and

[1] *Layman's Lent.*

"thou" in church may be good (or again it may not be), but when I realized that I could say "you" to God, and that I could talk to him in an ordinary conversational way, it added greatly to the reality of my prayers. As a young man I once had to meet a very important person whom I was anxious to impress. As I was talking to him, I became aware—but I couldn't stop myself—that I was speaking in a stilted fashion, with a special accent for the occasion, and that I was saying things which were just not "me". Children sometimes do this when they talk to adults. I often used to do it to God in my prayers, but I am now sure that he prefers me to be myself, though of course he wants to alter this self of mine as we go along.

The second characteristic of these prayers is that they are mostly concerned with the here and now. They begin with the question: What is most on my mind at the moment? Is it a work problem, the sickness of someone near to me, a happy event to which I look forward, the moon-landing, or the group area removals? Modern prayer is often criticized for this emphasis, because it seems to exclude all thoughts of God's transcendence; but I can only say that it doesn't do this for me. In any case it would equally be wrong to think of God as only transcendent.

Thirdly there is, in most of these modern writers, a clear distinction between God as he appears in our neighbour and in life-situations, and God as he is addressed in prayer. This distinction is criticized by Bishop Robinson as being "devotional Don Camillo, with 'the Lord' always around, as a ... friend at the side." There is a valuable warning here that this type of prayer could become just a cosy chat between me and God; he and I—just the two of us—talking about other people and together putting the world to rights. But I have not been able to avoid making this distinction. If God is completely identified with the scene of which we are a part, I do not see how we can escape humanism and pantheism. Christ, whom I see in the street and the bioscope, has already been seen by me in scripture and sacrament, and recognized as divine and transcendent. I do not begin to explain how this can be, but I believe that God, who is in the situation, is also other than, and beyond, the situation, and that is why I can pray to him as well as in him.

Fourthly in this sort of prayer I often find myself handing out information to God, rather on the lines of the old-fashioned meeting for extempore prayer, where we were invited to pray for the Christians in Chunking "which, Lord, as thou knowest, is in China".

I may imagine that I can get round this difficulty by the use of more sophisticated language, for instance, by putting the information in mental brackets. "Lord, I confess that (when I saw the mangled body of Joe Smith, auburn twenty-one year old university student) I did not feel sufficiently concerned (because doctors and ambulance men were there and I didn't know him anyway) and I did not even pray for him."

This, however, solves nothing. There is a prayer which does not hand out information to God. This is the prayer of listening, of silence, and of adoration. Perhaps that is the reason why these are the most profound of all our prayers.

Otherwise everything I say in prayer involves telling God something that he already knows. "Lord, I confess that I have murdered my aunt, robbed a bank, and eaten meat on Fridays." God is aware of what I have done, and perhaps all I need to say is: I confess. Yet God is our Father, and I have no doubt that he wants us to be open with him about all that is in our minds. In any case, *where a third party is concerned* (the reader of this book, the priest in the confessional, the members of a congregation), some amount of this sort of thing is inevitable, at least until we have progressed so far that only the prayer of silence can satisfy us.

But I wonder whether something is not happening here of which we may not be immediately aware. Is the source of this information in ourselves, or is it in God? Are we informing God, or is he informing us? Let me give an example. I sometimes write down prayers of this sort, and I now quote one exactly as I wrote it at the time:

Lord, this location, in a country dorp, was terribly shabby, broken down, and poor—not at all like the sophisticated locations of Johannesburg—and I don't know how the people live there. Just as I was leaving after the service, an old African woman gave me a rand note, saying that I must buy myself a cup of tea on the way home.

Lord, I had to take it, though it could have fed her whole family for a day. I had to take it, though a rand more or less does not mean much to me now. I had to take it, because it was a gift from you, a lesson in sacrificial giving, a humbling reminder that what counts with you is compassion.

I believe that such a prayer can be justified as it stands, as being a thinking over, in God's presence, of something that moved me at the time. But I believe that what I was really doing was to listen to God who was talking *to me* through the incident. So maybe I should re-write it as follows:

God speaks to me, and he says: Leslie, listen . . . Look at this dorp with my eyes, and see how terribly shabby and broken down it is. How do you suppose the people live there? Now look at this old woman whom I have sent to you. Take her gift, though it could have fed her whole family for a day. Take it, though you think in your superior way that you are indifferent to one rand more or less. Take it, for it is a gift from me, a lesson in sacrificial giving, a reminder that what counts with me is compassion.

Perhaps the most important contribution of modern spirituality is to make us listen to what God is saying to us, not only through the gospel and conscience, but through the world and through the people around us. And if we can learn how to listen, we shall inevitably be led on to the deeper prayers of silence and adoration.

# 3

## THE PRAYER OF LISTENING

Perhaps it is because I do not find that small talk comes easily to me that I am often irritated by the compulsive talker, the person who wants to dominate every conversation, to use ten sentences where one would do, and to turn every dialogue into a monologue. It is easy to criticize him and to feel superior to him. But it is not so easy to realize that this is what I myself so often do to God. The phrase "saying our prayers" is a revealing one. In our bedroom, in an arm-chair, as we walk along the street, we talk to God. We talk at God, whom we regard as a captive audience. We talk and talk, and when we have finished talking, we switch off our prayers without giving him a chance to get a word in edgeways. If I may put it in human terms, God must often be bored to distraction by the non-stop talking of my prayers.

This is one of the reasons why in the past I have often found prayer difficult and discouraging. If I dial my own telephone number, I get the engaged signal. If I am simply talking to myself in prayer, I am in the same position as the radicals about whom we thought in the first chapter. And unless I can hear God speaking, I cannot be sure that I am not talking only to myself in prayer.

I have found that the remedy for this is to spend much more prayer-time in listening to God. There are various ways in which this can be done.

First we can listen to what God says to us directly through the bible, through sermons and similar channels, and through our conscience. This imposes the absolute necessity of practising silence in prayer. After reading something out of the Bible, for instance, I must keep quiet and listen to what God is saying to me through those words. The other day I read: "Judge not, that you be not judged." After listening to them, I suddenly realized that I had been judging a man who had secretly spread some quite false accusations about me. Because of what he had done, I had had hard thoughts about him. From a worldly point of view, I had a right to judge him, but God was telling me that this is not the Christian way. When this happened I heard no tremendous voice from the sky speaking to me, but all the same it was God's voice and I had to stop and listen.

Although it is in scripture that we can most certainly hear the voice of God, my aim is to listen for it in everything that I read. This applies not only to "serious reading", but also to novels, newspapers, and magazines. In our day it is becoming increasingly realized that God speaks to us through the "secular" as well as through the "sacred" page.

The same applies to what God says to us through conscience. Sometimes it is quite simple to listen here. If I am tempted to embezzle church funds, my conscience will tell me, Don't do this thing—and it requires only a moment's reflection to realize that that was the voice of God. But at other times a considerable effort is required. Not long ago I met someone whom I had not seen for years. Some time back we had had to work together, and we had had a major disagreement about policy. Although we tried to deal with this in a Christian way, it was an awkward and unpleasant time for us both. Then when I met this man again, he grinned at me and said: "Have you forgiven me?" I said: "Of course I have." I thought that I was sincere in saying that, for I certainly bore him no resentment, but afterwards I found myself thinking: "Thank God I don't have to work with you again!" I might not have given another thought to this, but when I brought the incident into my prayer, I heard God saying to me through my conscience: "You haven't forgiven him, you know."

As we listen to God in this way, it is possible that he may

give us the answers to questions that we have asked him, and it is possible that he may answer our appeals for help. I find that he is more likely to speak to me of quite different things, about which I had not thought of asking him. It is this that makes prayer so interesting and exciting.

Besides listening to what God says through "religious" channels, we can also listen to what he says through the circumstances of our daily life and through other people.

> Lord, I confess to impatience with this impatient city, where the cars are hooting all day long—if the car in front delays for a second before moving at the robot, if another car looks like cutting in, if a pedestrian is too slow about crossing the road, or even for no reason at all, as far as I can see.

> Lord, today a car hooted at me and, when I looked round in annoyance, there was a car-load of friends smiling delightedly at being able to wave to me.

> Lord, I thank you for all joyful and friendly sounds. Help me to understand that these—and not the sounds of anger—are what matter most in this life.

In order to pray in this way, the everyday affairs of life have to be brought into prayer. Some people have the curious idea that this is wrong. They say: If in my prayer time I think about the behaviour of people in motor-cars, this is a distraction, something that takes my mind off God. So far from this being the case, I believe that God has a lot to do with motor-cars and the people in them, and that he speaks to us in this sort of way.

The incident may be less ordinary. While I was preaching to a packed congregation in a location church, a woman of the type that is always present in any of our location choirs— good-looking, sophisticated, and well dressed—rushed towards me and said, "I am sorry, but do you realize that the church is on fire?" And indeed it was, for an acolyte's candle had set some hangings alight and, but for her prompt action, this might have resulted in a general conflagration.

24

Lord, I confess that in my youth I thought that this was the right thing to do—to extinguish fire as soon as it appeared in church, since enthusiasm, pentecostalism, or anything of that sort, is unseemly in an Anglican.

Lord, now I wish for the fire, though still fearing the fire, and I rarely find it in the Church of the Province of South Africa. Make us all ready to be set on fire with love for you.

Here is another example from a film in which I saw a man organizing a crime with superb skill, confidence, and coolness. The crime succeeded in so far as the gang were willing to do exactly as he instructed. It failed when some of them began to pursue their own plans rather than his, to look to their personal profit rather than to that of the group, and to quarrel with each other.

Lord, I thank you that in real life you are running your Church with superb skill, confidence, and coolness. The Church succeeds in so far as we do exactly as you instruct us. Forgive our failures which are due to human self-trust in planning, to selfish ambition, and to lack of charity.

Lord, I pledge myself again today to obey your instructions to the letter, even when I cannot see the point of them, and to try to put my personal interests second to those of my fellows.

My last example comes from another ecclesiastical milieu. I had been deconsecrating a church. In the dusk, by candle-light because the electric current had been cut off, with a cold wind rattling the dilapidated windows, the two church-wardens, the rector, and I read evensong. We gave thanks for God's mercies received in this place, and then I read the deed of deconsecration. The old caretaker fluttered around like the ghost of some past worshipper.

Lord, what were we trying to do? I hear you saying that

seventy years ago we gave this building to you, and now you have returned it to us to throw away for you— not because of the rottenness of the woodwork (which could be repaired) but because it is empty, and there are hardly any parishioners left to use it now.

Lord, I have been consecrated. It would be terrible if you gave me back to myself, not because of my spiritual rottenness (which you could repair), but because my whole life was empty of compassion and care for others.

Lord, I thank you for the warning, and I ask that you will so fill me with your love that I may belong to you always.

There is, I agree, a possible danger in all this. Sometimes, when people think they are listening to God, they are in fact listening only to their own imagination. They try to make their minds an empty slate on which God will write a message, and then they receive surprising revelations and hear improbable voices. Particularly if we have a strong imagination, we should take care not to strain in any way to hear what God is saying, and we should not expect astonishing answers. When God has something to say to us, he is quite capable of getting it through to us if we have even one ear open for his words.

Besides listening in prayer to what God says to us in these different ways, I find that it is also possible just to listen. We can listen without getting, or even hoping to get, any messages from God, without getting any instructions or anything else from God.

We can listen to someone who is in distress and who comes to pour out his problems to us. We can listen to someone who is lonely and who wants another person to talk to. This is surely one of the things that the Lord meant by the parable of the sheep and the goats. "I was sick and you visited me, I was a stranger and you took me in." When we listen to people like that, we are listening to Christ.

This is true only if we really listen, but often we give not more than half our attention to what is said, or we are too busy to let the other man ramble on until he reaches the point. There is a ministry of listening, and the object of it is simply to listen to Christ who is present in those who are in need.

Sometimes I am tempted to complain that God doesn't hear me, but I know that this is complete nonsense. God always hears me. What we should be concerned about is whether we are able to hear him. It is generally my own fault when I fail to do so. One day I could not get any water to flow through the tap in my vestry. I rang up the plumber who found that someone, perhaps the gardener, had turned off the outside tap. I felt a fool, because I could easily have turned on that tap myself, if I had known what the trouble was.

So we say that nothing comes through to us from God, but it may well be that we ourselves, by our incessant talking, have turned off the tap. Those who are like what I used to be, and still sometimes am, a non-stop talker in their prayers, should try to be quiet and listen; and then they will hear what God has to say to them.

# 4

## PRAYER AND OUR DAILY CONCERNS

I have so far assumed that I am writing for people who pray more or less regularly at home, or who at least intend to do so, and I am suggesting that the "new" way of prayer might have something to offer them.

But we do not get very far in discussing personal prayers before we are asked why we should say them at all. I had better put my cards on the table at this point. I can never remember a time, from my earliest youth, when I doubted the importance or the relevance of prayer. There have been periods when for weeks on end I said no prayers at all, and felt various degrees of guilt at not doing so. There have been times when my prayers were on the wrong lines, as when I made a bargain with God that, if he would grant me success in a certain examination, I would be a pretty good Christian from then onwards. I have been disappointed when I have handed in shopping lists to God and he has not delivered the goods. In the early years of my priesthood I knew perfectly well what the pattern of a disciplined prayer life should be for me, but more often than not I let it go by the board through activism or sloth. Yet it has never seriously occurred to me that I needed to justify to myself the practice of personal prayer.

I say all this because my limitations should be understood.

Lord, in one sense I envy an atheist who has fought his way to belief in you, and I envy a man for whom prayer was at one time impossible, but who then discovered how to pray; for such people are more likely than I am to be able to assist those who are in doubt. Yet I

28

cannot help thanking you for always maintaining in me a desire to pray.

Lord, I listen to a schoolmaster telling me that he has given up prayer because it is boring, but how can it be boring if it brings us into touch with you?
I listen to a priest telling me that there is some meaning in corporate prayer, because it is an expression of our fellowship, but how can there be a duty to pray privately? And I ask: How can I have a "duty" to talk to someone whom I love?

Lord, it is easy to be judgmental about all this, and to fancy myself superior in some way to those who find problems about prayer. What I want to do is to express my penitence for failing to use better the immense benefits which you have—for no merits of mine—bestowed upon me.

As far as I can make out, what Jesus says to us in the gospel is not that we should discuss the idea of prayer, or debate whether prayer works, but that we should pray. I believe that we learn to pray as we go along. This is the way we learned to walk—not waiting until we could pass an examination on the theory of human locomotion, but just—by walking.

There was a time when I thought that prayer was viable only in certain conditions. I liked a church to pray in, and preferably one where the sacrament was reserved. I needed quiet and leisure in the early morning. I appreciate those conditions as much as ever, but I know now that it is no good waiting for the ideal. One of the Lord's deepest prayers was that in Gethsemane, where the conditions were very far from ideal.

One of the things that has helped me to pray in places and at times that I should have once thought unsuitable is the conviction which has grown over the years that the ordinary concerns of life must become subjects of prayer. I used to think that the only right way of meditating, for instance, was to start with the Bible, and let it suggest words in which I could communicate with God, as if he and I were alone in the world. I still generally start with the Bible, but now I find it easier to remember that God is concerned with everything that goes on. In giving some more examples from my own prayers, I have no illusions that these are in the Abbé Quoist class. It is because they are so ordinary that they may be of help to others.

The first one is called Noise. There have been so many noises today—buzz-bikes, sirens, a helicopter, dogs barking, carpenters sawing, workmen knocking out glass. They have disturbed me and made it hard for me to get on with my work, though I am sure that the noise-makers had no idea that they were doing that.

> Lord, I am sorry that I so often disturb you with the noises that I make. I don't do it deliberately to interfere with your work. At the time I am generally so self-centred that I have no idea what a noise I am making.

> But, Lord, the noises are there—the nagging worry about something that I have to do, the bubbling up of anger because an expensive repair job has proved ineffective, the shrill demands by which I attract attention to myself.

> Lord, give me interior silence, so that I can hear what you are saying. As for exterior silence, show me when to keep quiet, when to speak, and when it is right to make a noise.

If I think of prayer as being something out of this world, I end up by failing to get from prayer the strength to live my life in this world. It has been said that lives can be transfigured when cares are turned into prayers.

The second example arose out of an experience which led me to some words of the gospel. I met a coloured man at the door of the church. "May I speak to you?" he asked. I said "Yes," grudgingly because I wondered, "What is he going to ask me for? The fare to Germiston? The price of a night's lodging?"

> Lord, you said that you were a stranger whom we should take into our home. But I am suspicious of strangers of this sort, because I expect them to make demands upon me or to do me down in some way. Grant me a welcoming heart, for there is something of you even in those who do want to do me down.

> Then, Lord, this coloured man said: Please tell me how I can give myself more completely to Jesus. He has saved me from my sins, and I don't gamble or drink any more, but I must go deep, very deep, into what he wants for me. Although I am not an Anglican, may I use your church for prayer and Bible-reading during my lunch hour?

> Lord, I was ashamed of my suspicions, and humbled by his simplicity.

> Lord, it was I who was the stranger, and this man had welcomed me into the home of his faith.

The next one has a similar origin, but its meaning did not fall into place until later, when I was reading the Bible. On the way to Communion one day, I saw dustmen loading refuse on to their truck, cleaners emptying waste-paper baskets, and dirty scribblings on the walls of a lift—all contrasting vividly with the spotless altar to which I was going.

> Lord, you showed me what this meant when I read the words that you spoke after Judas had gone out to betray you: Now is the Son of Man glorified—*now*, when the dirt had been cleared out of the upper room, *now* your Godhead would be revealed.

> Lord, you are utterly separate from sin, yet at Bethlehem

31

you deliberately came down into the dirt, into the scum of society.

Lord, I ask you two things. With my whole heart I ask you to get rid of the dirt and the rubbish that clutters up my life. With some at least of my heart I ask you to strengthen me, that I may be ready to go down into any dirt for the redemption of souls whom you love.

The fourth prayer does not arise out of the Bible, but from reflection on prayer, which is also a part of our experience. We may think of our prayers as coming out of the "secret place", but this place is secret only in the sense that we do not generally advertise our prayers in the way that I am doing now. The effects of our prayer, and of our failure to pray, may well be no secret to others.

Lord, when I try to be a thankful Christian, I find that most of my thanksgivings contain a "but".

I thank you for plentiful possessions, but this reminds me that I ought to give more away.

I thank you for my health, but I wish that I hadn't this cold.

I thank you that I am a Christian, but this brings me many problems.

Lord, is this because my thanksgivings are insincere? Is it because, in my heart, I think that much more is due to me? Or is it because life is like this, and true happiness is to be found in suffering?

Lord, I will try to thank you also for the things that I have to suffer.

Here is another one on a life-theme. For much of our time we are necessarily concerned with other people, and our duty to these neighbours is an essential part of our religion.

Lord, you expect me to drink a lot of tea for your glory, and to eat many things that I would prefer not to eat.

Lord, today in this African rectory they had prepared an elaborate breakfast, going to great trouble and probably spending more than they could afford. I ungraciously said—what is true—that I never have more than coffee or tea and toast or bread for breakfast. Most unobtrusively everything except these things was removed from the table, and the priest and the schoolmaster—I know that the latter was looking forward to his breakfast—had just tea and bread with me.

Lord, I was humbled by this act of fellowship and consideration, as I was humiliated by my failure in tact.

Lord, grant me grace to accept whatever is set before me, much or little, attractive or indifferent.

All I am suggesting here is that I now know that daily concerns must find a place in my prayers, and I do not mean that this style is the only way in which it can be done. Nor is there any reason why others should write out their prayers. I find it helpful, and have done it in one form or another for ten years. Perhaps I am a compulsive writer, but I find that to write something down is a check against day-dreaming.

If it is felt that these prayers are too familiar, too concerned with the immanence of God, I agree that prayers are imperfect if they are lacking in awe and praise, and I shall have something to say about that later on.

c

# 5

## INTERCESSION

Some of my friends retain far more vivid recollections of their early childhood than I do. They can remember how they learned to pray and what first made prayer real for them. I know that I was taught to pray when I was very small, especially at bedtime, and that at an early age I was brought in for family prayers. (This is a custom which unfortunately has almost died out among Europeans, though in African homes it is still often practised.) My guess is that the reality of prayer first came to me when I could understand something of what it meant to say: God bless mummy and daddy.

I wonder whether Jesus said that prayer when he was a little boy at Nazareth? Certainly as he grew up, he often prayed for others, and I do not know where, humanly speaking, he would have learned to do so unless his mother had taught him. If at some time in his adolescence she told him about the circumstances of his birth, this could have made such an impression upon him as almost to dictate the shape of the Lord's Prayer. Our Father (Father of Mary and all of us), who art in heaven (from where Gabriel came to Mary), hallowed be thy name (as Mary feared and adored you), thy kingdom come (the kingdom that Gabriel promised), thy will be done (as Mary had said: Be it unto me according to your word). The petition for daily bread could have come from a time when cash was short in the home and Mary prayed for bread just for today. Her forgiveness of those who gossiped cruelly about her, her temptation to doubt that the child she had borne could be the Son of God, her deliverance from evil during the time of the flight to Egypt were, I expect, subjects that she also turned into prayer.

Anyway, in the public ministry we hear Jesus praying for Peter, that his faith might not fail; for all his disciples, that the Father would protect them and keep them united; and for his enemies on the cross. And we are told that in heaven he is continually making intercession for us.

I find it hard to see how any Christian could not wish to follow his example. If we have no place in our prayers for others, it seems to me that we show ourselves up as self-centred. Yet Christians often complain that they find it hard to intercede.

In my young days we were always taught that we must have lists of people to pray for, lists for a week, lists for a month, lists for special occasions such as the ember days, parish lists, diocesan lists. It was all extremely complicated, and we were dependent on having the right piece of paper handy at the right time. I am sure that there is value in having some sort of a simple list, for otherwise with a memory as inadequate as mine I should forget a considerable number of people for whom I want to pray. But the list should not be an end in itself, as I find it becoming if I just read it through and then say an Our Father. It is only an *aide-memoire* to ensure that my intercessions are as wide as possible.

When we have decided, in whatever way, for whom we are going to pray, how should we set about it? One way is to talk to God about them as naturally as possible, and see where the conversation takes us. Here, for instance, is a prayer for the hungry, written in Hunger Week, when we had been asked to give up one meal a day as an act of intercession for those who have not enough to eat.

Lord, I thank you that you have always given me my daily bread. I have never really been hungry. The other day I had to wait three hours beyond my normal time for supper, and I complained of hunger; which was absurd.

Lord, this is Hunger Week, and on Monday I forgot all

35

about it, and had an extravagant, but delicious, sole meunière for lunch, at a price which would have fed a whole family in Soweto. And I think of our theological students in Grahamstown who, every Friday throughout the year, not only go without lunch, but have the lunch cooked and sent to African homes in the location.

Lord, I am sorry for the hungry when I think about them, but I do not care deeply enough. This applies to so many other things too. Lord, it applies even to you. I do care for you, but often I forget you.

Lord, give me grace to hunger and thirst for you, and to deny myself for the sake of my suffering brethren.

Sometimes our own experience suggests ways of praying for others. One night I could not get to sleep for some hours. This was unusual for me, and I thought it a great deprivation, until I remembered to thank God for sleep, which I had assumed to be my right.

Lord, as I lie awake, I think of the non-sleepers,
    those who watch, weep, and mourn to-night,
    those who cannot sleep because they are torn by anxiety,
    the sick in hospital,
    the night workers,
    the night travellers,
    thieves and those on unlawful errands.

Lord, I think of you sleepless in Gethsemane, sleepless during the hidden hours of Good Friday, continuing all night in prayer, walking on the water in the third watch of the night.

Grant, Lord, that awake we may watch with you, and in sleep may take our rest.

Charles Péguy[1] says that it is possible to pray without realizing that we are doing so:

[1]*God Speaks*, p. 82.

God says: But I hear them. Those obscure impulses of the heart, the obscure and good impulses, the secret good impulses,

Which unconsciously soar up, which are born and unconsciously ascend towards me,

And he in whose breast they originate is not even aware of them, he doesn't know about them, he is only the originator,

But I collect them, says God, and I count them and weigh them.

I am sure that this is true. We unconsciously pray for others when we think about them, and when we desire to help them. Once I had been interviewing ordination candidates, and I was discussing them with a friend. We were not merely gossiping or criticizing, but we were trying to see who among them was suited to be a minister, considering both the benefit of the church and the best interests of the man himself.

Is it this one, who is unstable, but who has a deep sense of his own unworthiness?

Or that one, who has charm and good looks in such abundance that all the girls would swoon at the sight of him in a clerical collar?

Or he who, until he is free from the apron-strings of his girl-friend, cannot tell what he wants to do?

Or the one of whose academic brilliance there is no doubt, but is he too withdrawn to be able to help others?

Or the patient plodder who would make a perfect curate, but what would he do if in charge of a parish?

Or the rebel, who would infuriate us in his early days, but who might turn out to be the best leader of them all?

When we were talking like this, we were not praying in the strict sense of the word, but our discussion was in fact a prayer. Yet it is always good if we can pull this sort of thing

37

together, and give it shape by bringing prayer consciously into it. Perhaps in this instance we could have said:

> Lord, show us which of these should be chosen, and how they can best be guided. Even if you don't want any of them to be ordained, make them all your faithful disciples. Develop their good gifts, and overcome in them their weaknesses.

In praying for others, one thing to be constantly looked for is the chance of doing something to help them. Sometimes there seems to be nothing that we can do, as when we pray for the sufferers in the Vietnam war. But when we pray for those with whom we are in contact, we must make sure that prayer is not a substitute for compassion. I have prayed for that man, so I have fulfilled my duty towards him. Simon Phipps says that the cheque-book and the intercession list are the two greatest insulators against commitment.

One of our priests who is under discipline wrote to tell me that he could not get a job, that he was practically starving, he and his wife getting at most one meal a day, and that he felt his life to be futile.

> Lord, I thought I was making a generous response by arranging for some money to be sent to him, and for some parish chores to be given to him, so that he should not feel entirely a recipient of "charity".

> Then, Lord, I started to prepare a sermon on: Does God care? And I realized that this is not the sort of caring that you go in for. Until I have given myself to this man in his humiliation, as you gave yourself to me on the cross, I have not begun to care.

> Lord, I am going to see him, and I ask you to show me how I should approach him.

Unless I am careful, I find my intercessions being narrowed down to those I most care about. I am sure, for instance, that I criticize the government more often than I pray for them. The work of the Church in lands other than our own

38

(and if we are not interested in the Church of some other land, it is time that we found such an interest) is a must. The people whom we meet casually should be remembered as well as those who work with us. Where possible, I pray for people by name.

Enclosed communities, who give much time to prayer for others, not only organize their intercessions but also are wide open to the needs of the world. "Intercessions as they come in are all entered—those for people with whom we are permanently connected in one book, each day of the week having its special intentions, and those for urgent or temporary needs with their letters in another; a summary of the news in *The Times* is written every morning in a third book, commonly known as 'World News'. These books are kept on the Watch desk."[1]

> Lord, I talked much about the dispute in the Middle East, but I confess that I scarcely prayed for peace until the fighting had actually started. This may have been because I did not think there was a serious danger of war, but more probably it was because my feelings were not involved.

> Then, Lord, I had tea with a Rabbi and, in his book-lined study, I saw his wife teaching their fourteen year old son to read in the Torah. I sensed their deep concern for their people in Israel, and I knew that, if the boy had been three years older, he would have been off to the war.

> Lord, give me the imagination to see that international events and crises always mean people, the death or life of people, the uplifting or deterioration of people, the joy or sorrow of people.

There are many problems connected with praying for individuals. We can be too vague—God bless my friend—or we can be too definite. A certain tycoon is one of the people I want to pray for and, as I think about him, I cannot avoid

[1]*Mother Millicent*, by Sister Felicity Mary S.P.B., p. 79.

remembering that he has on occasion a foul temper. So it seems natural for me to pray that he may be given a bigger share of patience. But this means in fact that I am sitting in judgment upon him, for I have looked on his weakness and then asked God—in a way that makes me feel smug—that he may improve and become in fact rather more like me!

There are two possible ways of dealing with this situation. When I am aware of the sins or weaknesses of the person for whom I am praying, I can identify myself in some way with him.

> Lord, look mercifully on this man, who is being reclaimed from alcoholism. He is going straight now and doing much good work. But he is resentful at not being allowed to handle his own money, which would be fatal to him.

> Lord, look mercifully on me your unworthy servant, who can scarcely claim even that I do much good work, I am often resentful because it is not possible for me to have many things that I think I ought to have, not understanding that they would be bad for me.

> Lord, take away our blindness and make us realize that you are already giving us, with great generosity, all the things that are good for us to have.

Here again, I do not specifically ask God to bless the man in some particular way, but this is implied in a prayer that I offer for us both as we cry out from the ditch of our common humiliation. From a similar situation comes a prayer about doubt.

> Lord, this priest tells me that, although he still believes in you as saviour, he doesn't know whether he believes anything else, so he wants to renounce his orders, and perhaps his membership of the church.

> Lord, I thank you that you have given me a confident faith—however badly I practise it—in the divine institution of your Church and in my priesthood,

whereas so many men, who are better than I am, are filled with doubts.

Lord, save me from being superior or impatient with doubters. I believe that all genuine and fearless search for truth has your blessing, for you are the truth. Perhaps if I were stripped of all the comfortable appurtenances with which my faith is accompanied I too should be more of a doubter.

My other way of interceding is through the words of scripture, and this is especially valuable when I want to pray for someone, but I am not sure how to set about it. If we use the words of scripture we cannot go wrong. "Our Father—her Father and mine—glorify your name in her, your kingdom come in her, your will be done by her. Give her today her daily bread, and forgive her her sins, as may she forgive those who sin against her. Save her from the time of trial, and deliver her from evil." What better prayer could I pray for her than that?

In the same kind of way I sometimes use the Beatitudes, asking all those happinesses for the person I am praying for. The sermon on the mount, the epistles of St Paul, especially that to the Philippians, and the last discourses of St John, also supply a lot of suitable material. So do the classical prayers of the Christian tradition, for example: "Soul of Christ sanctify him"; or "O Saviour of the world, by your cross and passion you have redeemed them; save them and help them, I humbly beseech you, O Lord".

Even if I am satisfied—which I rarely am—that I am spending as much time as I could on intercession, and that I am using that time as well as I could, this is a little thing compared with the great volume of prayer which, I know, is being offered by others for me. I suppose that most Christians have had the experience of facing an insoluble problem, or making a difficult decision, or getting through some agonizing suffering, which seemed impossible before it happened, and then easy when the time came. Looking back afterwards, it was hard to doubt that we had been greatly helped by those who were praying for us. I find that this fact of being interceded for is a spur to my own intercession.

There are also the prayers of the saints and, far more wonderful than these, the prayers of Jesus himself. Our poor intercessions are joined to his, and this is the only ultimate reason why they have any value or importance.

# 6

## THANKSGIVING

I have heard it said that the real reason why the British were turned out of India was that they had never learned how to say thank you. This could also be the reason why the white man has been turned out of so many parts of Africa, for we delude ourselves when we say that it is only the Africans who are ungrateful. The essence of thanksgiving is an acknowledgment of our dependence, and the reason why we are bad at it is quite simply our pride.

Lord, in my folly I often think that what I have I deserve to have. I have worked hard for it. My ability has put me where I am. This is my right.

Lord, I go further than this, and think that I should be the most important person in every situation in which I find myself; the whole world really ought to be ordered according to my convenience.

Lord, this is why, when things go wrong and I do not get my deserts, I grumble and complain and am miserable.

Lord, all this is pride, and I know that pride must be humbled. You have told me that the remedy for pride is thanksgiving. If I had a truly thankful heart, I should know that I deserve to have nothing at all. I cannot help doing some things well, and knowing that I have done them well, but this is all right if I realize that my gifts come from you and that the most I can do is to receive them humbly and gratefully.

If we ask what are the things for which we should especially thank God, the answer is—everything. Of course there are times when gratitude springs up spontaneously, and the only thing to watch here is that it should be directed specifically to God. For instance, it was a moving experience to preside one day at a eucharist for the deaf and dumb. I preached on thanksgiving, and I found it easy to be thankful there.

> Lord, I thanked you first (and I realized that I was being selfish in putting this first) that you allow me to hear and to speak.

> Lord, I thanked you also that you have, through the chaplain's expertise, allowed your Church to minister so well to these people. That they could understand and follow the service was as great a miracle as when you said "Ephphatha".

> Lord, I thanked you above all for the devotion and cheerfulness of these people, who had so courageously overcome their handicap.

But very often—perhaps more often than not for those of us whose pride is so deep-seated that we are not obviously thankful persons—it does not come naturally to be grateful. In fact we do not value our happiness until something takes it away.

> Lord, it didn't occur to me to be thankful for my health until I fell ill; or for my friends until I found myself alone; or for my sanity until I saw mental cases in padded cells; or for my safety until terrorism drew near; or for my redemption until I felt the need for forgiveness.

> Lord, make me thankful for all things at all times.

> Lord, these farmers were complaining about the long drought and the bad harvest. They said there would be starvation this year. When they were asked whether they had remembered to thank God last year for the good harvest, they said: No, we were too busy eating the mealies.

44

Lord, make me thankful for all things at all times.

Our obligation to thank God for food, by saying grace before meals, is often forgotten nowadays. When it would be embarrassing to do so publicly, I try to say it privately. It may seem a little matter, but it helps me to show gratitude at regular intervals during the day. In order to avoid formalism I try to vary the words of grace as often as possible. If only I could enjoy a large breakfast, I should use this one:

> For bacon, eggs, and buttered toast,
> Praise Father, Son and Holy Ghost.

But if we are going to thank God at all times for all things (Eph. 5.20), a conscious effort is needed to ensure a regular place for this in our thoughts and prayers. Some find that their evening prayers are mainly taken up with thanking God for the good things that have happened to them that day. As I am generally too sleepy to say any significant prayers at night, I try to introduce some thanksgivings into every period that I set apart for prayer. I suppose that, if I could preserve a spirit of thanksgiving all day long, there would be no need for that.

I remember a sermon preached by Canon Streeter in my college chapel at evensong many years ago. His theme was that, on every day of our lives, we should find some new thing for which to thank God. Most of his sermon was taken up with giving us examples of the sort of things to be grateful for. He became increasingly enthusiastic about these, ignored the clamour of the dinner trumpet, and preached far into the night. Though we were not amused at the time, he was obviously right. If we really begin to "count our blessings", a life-time is too short to complete the process.

> Thank you, Lord, for the jacarandas that have been so beautiful this year—a low blue cloud hanging over Westcliff.
> Thank you for the unearthly wonder of the lightning which comes almost every evening now.
> Thank you for the reverence of the students at the

mid-day Eucharist, and for the high-school girls who really seemed to enjoy their religious service today.

Thank you for that young woman who felt free to talk to me about her personal problems.

There is also thanksgiving for the more obviously spiritual things, for prayer which opens up heaven for us, for faith which gives meaning to life, for the sacraments which keep us going in our needs and problems, for our unity in Christ.

Lord, I thank you for the Eucharist which is Thanksgiving, but first I thank you for making me a Christian, when so many better people than I am have no faith. I don't know why you have done this, but thank you, Lord.

Lord, I thank you for the Thanksgiving, but first I thank you for the worshipping community, which makes it possible for me to plead the holy sacrifice. If I were the only Christian in Johannesburg, I don't know how long I could last.

Lord, I thank you for the Thanksgiving, but first I thank you, who are the abiding life of the Church. We often imagine that the Church is something which we keep going, but it is all yours, Lord, all yours.

St Paul says that thanksgiving is in fact a test of whether something is good or bad. We cannot thank God for a thing that we know to be evil. But if there is something for which we could thank him, something that is at least capable of being sanctified by the word of God and prayer (1 Tim. 4.4), that thing is good. Unless thanksgiving is a normal part of our life it will not, however, occur to us to make this test.

In spite of our selfishness, it should not be very difficult to thank God for the good things that we receive—provided that our life is on the whole a happy one, as mine is. But what about those people whose life is, on balance, marked more by sorrow than by joy? What of the young mother who is dying of cancer, the soldier who knows that he is unlikely to escape from the jungles of Vietnam, the child who, even if he recovers from kwashiorkor, will never have a chance in life? Do we expect them also to be full of thanksgiving?

But even if our life is set in pleasant places and we are happy people, we all have something to suffer. Are we going to regard all suffering as something which alienates us from God, and so makes it impossible for us to thank him?

Lord, help me to remember how St Paul rejoiced in his sufferings, and gloried in his infirmities; and how St Peter told those who were going through great trials to rejoice, inasmuch as they were partakers of your sufferings.

Lord, with my mind I can recognize that to thank you for the unpleasant things that happen to me would be right, because this would draw me nearer to you in your passion. Yet with my heart I am rarely loving enough to do so—at least at the time. Perhaps afterwards I can look back and be grateful for some suffering which has helped me.

But, Lord, at least I can thank you that you are with me in my trouble.

If we have not learned to thank God in the joyful times, we shall certainly not do so in the sorrowful ones, so we had better practise thanksgivings for minor sufferings, that we may be prepared to go on thanking God even if major sufferings follow.

The great thing, then, is to thank God always and for everything through the Eucharist, in prayers at set times, in a habit of thanksgiving. But this is more than a matter of words, for we must also have a thankful heart.

I once gave a lift in my car for some considerable distance to an old African. When I put him down, he just drifted off, without even saying goodbye. I hope I didn't say anything about African ingratitude, though I may have been tempted to do so. He was a simple, illiterate man who knew no better, so I soon forgot the incident. Some weeks later he came to see me, and he brought me a live chicken as a present. Even now he could find no words to express what he felt, but he merely said, "I have brought you a chicken".

> Lord, a smooth-tongued man would have pleased me by making a beautiful speech at the end of the journey, but it need not have meant anything at all. I thank you for this old man, who taught me how to put gratitude into action.

> Lord, grant me to show gratitude by my words, by a continually joyful spirit, and by giving up my life to your service.

As a footnote to all this, I recall that the Pharisee in the parable was a great expert in thanksgiving, and he got no marks at all from the Lord. This was because his thanksgiving—which was all right as far as it went—was basically selfish and lacking in love. I gather from this that no one form of prayer is complete in itself. Thanksgiving must take its place as one aspect of that total commitment which is the total life of prayer.

# 7

## PETITION

Jesus tells us to ask for things in prayer, and to go on asking in faith, without getting tired of doing so. To some people this is all quite straightforward. They are told to do it and they do it. They expect answers and they get answers. But there is much current doubt about the prayer of petition, and I can sympathize with this. As a child and a teenager, I went in for petition quite a bit, and then I found myself asking a lot of questions which for a time inhibited me from this sort of prayer.

Is it not a protestant way of praying? Surely catholics are taught to praise God and to adore him, rather than to be always running to him with requests?

If we ask God for things, are we not trying to make him change his mind? Am I not acting like a public relations officer, if I endeavour to persuade God to do something that originally he had no intention of doing?

If God really loves me, surely he will look after me without my having to remind him what to do all along the line? Did not Jesus himself say: "Your Father knows what things you have need of before you ask him?"

If God always gave me whatever I requested, would not the result be disastrous? This is certainly my belief, as I look back upon my own life.

Isn't this a selfish form of prayer? Supposing I pray that I should get a certain job, may I not obtain the job at the expense of someone who needs it more than I do, or who would do it better than I could? Isn't this sort of prayer a black-market method of getting what I want?

49

D

Is it even possible? Can I live in isolation, as if there were no other people in the world? Did not Jesus teach us to say, "Give *us* this day *our* daily bread"? Did he not say, "If *two* of you agree upon earth, as touching anything that they shall ask, it shall be done for them"?

It wasn't until I started from the other end that these questions fell into perspective for me. I still can't answer a lot of them, but I am now content to leave them unanswered and to get on with petition.

Lord, you are a great petitioner. You are always asking me for things—for prayer, time, sympathy, visits to the sick, letters, patience, money, truthfulness. If I tried to make a list of all that you ask me for it would never end.

Lord, sometimes I hear your clear request, and then I think that I can improve upon it. Sometimes I rebel and complain that your demands upon me are quite unreasonable, and how can you expect me to have the resources to do all these things? Sometimes I say that I will do the things you ask, and I do really intend to do them, but then something crops up to distract me and, like the man in the parable, I don't do them. Sometimes I know that you are asking me to do something about a certain situation, but I am not clear what it is that you want me to do. Your request has become distorted because I am not well enough trained spiritually to hear what you are saying.

Lord, if I behave like this, how can I have the nerve to ask anything from you? If I always answered your requests, I should feel better about making requests to you. I don't mean that I think you are a hard-hearted business man who will never give something for nothing. You are love, but in true love there is a two-way traffic, and I must do what you ask of me, as well as asking you for things.

Lord, when I really try to do what you ask—really try, in spite of many failures—that makes me feel better about asking you to help me. There is another thing, Lord. If I really did what you asked, I should become a more dedicated Christian. Then I should know better what are the right things to ask you for.

With this in mind as a background, I turn to the Bible and find that it encourages us to pray for specific things in a definite way. To take a few examples: Abraham's steward asked, "O Lord God, grant me success today." Hannah prayed for a child. The psalmist says: "Give me understanding"; "Deliver me from my enemies."

The Lord's own teaching is clear. When he tells us to pray for things, we can assume that he was not reading out of a book or broadcasting someone else's sermon, but that he was speaking from his own heart and experience. And this is what he said: "Ask and it will be given you; seek and you will find; knock and it will be opened to you. For everyone who asks receives." He went on to enquire what father gives a stone when his son asks for bread. Perhaps there is a childhood memory here of a father at Nazareth who, in contrast to Joseph, gave his child a stone or a snake, and of a child running away hungry and afraid. The heavenly Father is the giver of all good things.

It would be convenient if the New Testament included a manual which gave us precise directions as to how we should pray. It certainly does not do that, but there is one emphasis which is stressed above all others—and that is that petition is essential. We should therefore not be afraid to go on asking for things.

Later Jesus somewhat qualified his teaching by saying, "Whatever you ask in prayer, you will receive if you have faith." Some people believe that faith means working ourselves up into a state of near hysteria. The aeroplane is losing height. We have been told to fasten our seatbelts and warned that there may be trouble about landing. I pray: "O God, grant me a safe arrival;" and then I find myself willing God to grant me a safe arrival. I feel that, if I pray with enough faith, God will have no option. During the London air-raids in the last war, I thought that I had some faith, but I was surprised one day to find myself supposedly praying, and yet in fact willing the bomb that was coming down to fall on someone other than myself.

Faith means coming to the Lord, putting our lives into his hands, and doing what he tells us to do. To ask for things in perfect faith means to be so close to him in heart and mind and will that we ask only for those things for which he wants us to ask. "Whatever you ask *in my name* I will do it." It follows that God wants us to use this prayer of petition, but he warns us that we shall not be much good at it until we have learned what dedication means.

One of the reasons why this type of prayer is important is that it helps us to understand our creatureliness and dependence, to become little children as Jesus told us to. If I truly pray in this way I make myself a beggar. An apostolic "crank" once asked me if I prayed that I might receive my stipend at the end of the month. I replied: No—apart from often saying "Give us this day our daily bread"—because I *knew* that I should receive my cheque.

> Then, Lord, I got the message. How dare I assume that I should receive a stipend as if it was my right? Or my health or my friends or anything else at all? All these gifts come from your bounty and, if I am truly your child, I shall ask you for them.

> But, Lord, my one doubt is whether continual asking of this sort might not be a sign of a lack of confidence in you, a sign of worry, a desire to make sure that you don't forget me.

> Lord, help me to put aside the problems, and just ask, as a child asks, in simple trust.

I am sure that we must ask, and be specific, but always in a spirit of acceptance. After the Lord had prayed that the cup might pass from him, he went on to pray that "not my will but yours be done". The "I want" prayer has to be changed into the "your will be done" prayer, for all true prayer approximates to the conditions of Gethsemane.

> Lord, I have had a rushed and non-stop day, and now there are so many thoughts to excite my mind that I can't get to sleep.

> Lord, I say to you: What *I* should like is to go to sleep at once, to sleep deeply, and to wake up refreshed when the alarm goes.

> Lord, I tell you this because you love me, and I think you want me to tell you what I am feeling. But I don't want to order you to do this for me. I am willing to stay awake all night, if that is what you want.

> Lord, into your hands I commend my spirit.

But we must not suppose that it is enough to speak our prayers of petition. We must also enquire whether there is anything for us to do about the things prayed for.

> Lord, I thank you for this priest who, without renouncing his orders, has given up the full-time paid ministry, and taken a lay job. Most people do not understand what this is all about, and they imagine him holding lunch-hour services in the canteen, or else doing his real work in his spare time, in order to save the church a lot of money.

> Lord, I thank you that this man prayed, as we all pray, that the Church might bear witness and make contact in the places where men spend most of their waking hours; but that he wasn't content with praying. He saw that there was something that he could do about it, and he did it.

> Lord, when I ask for something, make me also consider whether there isn't something I can do about it; and make me strong to act as well as to pray.

Moreover, we should not be surprised—as I often am—when

God answers our prayer. An example of this is the ecumenical movement. We have for long been praying for unity, but we tend to be astonished when there are signs that God is answering our petitions, especially when he is bringing the Churches together along lines which we ourselves do not easily approve of.

I have always been fascinated by the Roman Catholic Church—at a distance. I have learned much from it. I have sometimes envied, hated, and feared it. I have often been put off but its seeming arrogance, its resentment against Anglicans, especially in Tanzania, and its desire to steal converts from us. Now all this has changed. Its local leaders treat me as a brother, they have no doubts about sharing in service and worship and witness, and many have openly said that they accept our orders as valid.

> Lord, I praise you for this transfiguration, and I see the face of the Roman Church shining like the sun; but it is really you whom I see transfigured. You have torn aside the human veils—or was it only my blindness which prevented me from seeing you through them?— and your glory now shines forth.

> Lord, it is a miracle, and I thank you for this answer to many prayers.

God in fact always answers our prayers. I find that he frequently does not give me the answers that I would like but, as the Dutch Catechism says, he always answers in the direction along which we ask, though *often at a higher level*. The Pharisees asked for the kingdom of God, and they got Jesus Christ. Jesus asked for the cup of the passion to be removed from him, and he got the resurrection. We ask for health, and get patience to endure suffering; we ask for money and power that we might enjoy life, and we are given life so that we can enjoy all good things; we ask for the gift of prayer, and we are given aridity, through which we learn to pray more deeply. None of our prayers is wasted. God uses them all in whatever way he thinks best.

# 8

## PENITENCE

Mary Blackburn was a remarkable woman who was aged 90 at the time that her book *Conversations on the Edge of Eternity* was published. She was brought up as an Anglican, but in middle age she left us for another religious body, because she thought that we teach a sin-centred religion. I am afraid that we do sometimes give that impression, but we ought not to do so, because at the heart of our faith is, not the sin of man, but the love of God. Repentance is our God-given response to this love.

> Lord, show me how I ought to look at my sin. I know that I often feel ashamed when I have failed to live up to my standards. I have done bad things which I hope other people didn't notice because, if they did, they would think less well of me. I have had my faults pointed out to me and felt only resentment at this.

> Lord, show me how to look at my sin. Unless I believe in you, I cannot talk about sin, but only about bad behaviour. It is when I look towards you, and see how my failings are an offence against your love, that I can begin to see what sin means.

Jesus was uninhibited in talking about sin. He saw an ultimate distinction between right and wrong, a distinction which, in this permissive age, we tend to blur, supposing that right and wrong somehow meet at infinity. For Jesus a sinner was like a man driving along a road in which, unknown to him, there was an enormous sink-hole. If he didn't pull up soon he would inevitably fall into what Jesus called "the damnation of hell". I find myself saying that I don't care for that phrase, but even when I translate it as "judgement", I cannot escape its meaning.

> Lord, I know that sin is serious, but I make excuses, both for myself and for others. There are physical and psychological reasons for behaving as we do. There are complementary virtues. I know that I shouldn't have done this, but you wouldn't send me to hell for a comparatively small thing like that, surely?

> Lord, does this mean that I have what Paul calls a depraved mind? If my hand is badly burned, I lose all sense of touch. If my mind is badly burned, I lose all sense of you. Make me more sensitive to you, in order that I may be more sensitive to my sins which wound you.

Jesus had no use for those who maintain that the only sins which matter are the obvious ones. I haven't murdered anyone, I don't commit adultery, I don't steal (or if I do, I take care that no one knows about it)—so I'm all right, Jack. But sin, according to Jesus, is something inside us. The real sins, therefore, are those that other people often know nothing about—the thoughts of pride and anger and selfishness, the willingness to compromise with truth, or to accept a standard which I know to be second-rate.

> Lord, some people travel around with an announcement on their cars that they have a tiger in their tank. But I have a tiger in my heart. My unconscious is a witches' cauldron, and there are unknown beasts within me which would emerge to produce terrifying anarchy, once the inhibiting bars were down. I know this from the consuming rages, the furious eagerness of imagination, the undisciplined thoughts, that often get half-way through the bars.

> Lord, I do not know why the tiger does not break loose. Is it that I want to be respected? That I haven't

enough nerve to let myself go? All I know is that there is rebellion within me, and that I am fighting against myself.

Lord, unless you kill this tiger, your victorious and unifying Easter life cannot properly express itself through me.[1]

A particular example of this hidden sin is seen in the Pharisees, who were highly respectable men, but lacking in positive goodness.

Lord, you didn't like the Pharisees, because they chose to live in an unreal world. They had to lie to themselves so that they might go on living in unreality. They were so self-deceived that they couldn't tell the difference between a camel and a mosquito. (I see you smiling as you said that.) They were blind, but they refused to have their cataract removed. They thought their righteousness was real, and that it was piling up celestial credit for them.

Lord, the reason why you liked blackmailers, publicans, and prostitutes was that they had no illusions. They lived in the real world and knew that they were sinners; and when you talked to them about salvation they understood what you were saying.

Lord, I hope I am not a pharisee, though I know that there is something of the Pharisee in me. I don't want to be a "publican", though I do want humble penitence. Let me think of sin as you thought of it.[2]

Another thing that Jesus said about sin was that many of the most serious sins are negative ones. In the Gospels he causes a parade of notorious sinners to pass before our eyes, and most of them would not normally be called sinners at all. There was the man who put his hand to the tractor and then looked back—the unreliable man, the nondescript Christian who

[1]Helmut Thielicke, *Life can begin again*, p. 42 f.
[2]T. R. Glover, *The Jesus of history*, p. 163 f.

does things by fits and starts. He says that such a man is *useless* in the kingdom of God. There was the man who hid money under the floor-boards instead of putting it in the Building Society. There were the girls who did nothing worse than forget to put new batteries into their torches—but they were sent to hell, you notice, while the dying gangster was promised paradise. The supreme example is found in the frightening parable of the sheep and goats. There we are told that in the last judgement we shall be asked, not whether we went to church and kept the commandments, or even whether we were Christians, but simply whether we went out of our way to help those who were in need. I know that I shall be astonished by the enormity of my sins of omission.

> Lord, is it morbid to go on talking like this about sin? I hear you answering me: Yes, my son, it is morbid if that is all that you do. You can recognize your sins and you can grovel in the dust because of them and, if you do no more than that, the end will be despair. Judas Iscariot recognized that his sins had betrayed me, and his reaction was suicide. But there is a fact which is infinitely greater than the fact of sin, and that is my forgiving love. My son, take the shutters down and open the windows of your life, not mainly so that you can see the dirt which is there inside, but so that my healing light may come in.

In all the frustration that sin often causes me, I try to hold on to this great fact of God's love. He died for us on the cross, and so released a power which is great enough to take away all our sins and reconcile us to him. But I sometimes forget that this is not an automatic process. A German philosopher once said, "I need not bother about my sins. Whatever they are, God will pardon me—that is his job." But the aim of Jesus at Calvary was not to create a utopia in which it was safe for sinners to go on sinning.

So there are three things to be done. First there must be a ruthlessly honest examination to find out what our sins really are. It is often easier to see other peoples' sins than my own.

A very tiresome woman was once explaining to me that she never went to confession because she had no "serious" sins to confess. I felt like saying: "Give me a piece of paper and I will write out your confession for you." It did not occur to me at the time that anyone who knew me well could write out my confession in a way that might astonish and disturb me. I hope that I am not unique in this, but the older I get the more I realize my capacity for self-deception. When St Paul says that he has opened his heart wide to the Corinthians, and asks them in exchange to do the same for him (2 Cor. 6.11–13 NEB), I take it that he is telling me to be open to receive from others what they think about me. Experience in leadership training groups in some respects makes it possible for this to happen. When, in the words of the psalmist, we ask God to cleanse us from our secret sins, to me at least it means not only those sins which I manage to keep secret from others, but also those which, though obvious to others, are a secret from myself.

The second thing is that we have to confess our sins to God. He is ready to forgive us even before we come to him, but we must confess if we are to accept his forgiveness into our lives.

There is no need here to enlarge upon the sacrament of penance, because the writing about it is endless. Sacramental confession is available, but not compulsory, for Anglicans. I myself have used it regularly for most of my life, and I do not know how I could have kept going without it. But its value is being much questioned in these days.

This is partly because people who go regularly to confession find that they are always confessing the same sins. Why I should expect to have a completely different set of sins every month I do not know. Satan is not particularly original, and if he finds that I am allergic to a certain temptation, it is not surprising that he should go on plaguing me with it. It only emphasizes the fact that sin is a supremely boring business.

It is partly because many of the sins confessed seem to be petty. If this really means that the soul has already got rid of the more "deadly" sins, it is something to be grateful for.

It is more likely to mean, however, that the root sins remain almost unrecognized. Sometimes it helps me to use an up-to-date list for self-examination, such as the one put out by St George's cathedral, Cape Town, which includes such questions as: "Do I get upset about unimportant trifles? Do I believe that only one newspaper tells the truth? Do I believe that I am indispensable?"

It is partly because more often than not we can feel no spiritual progress as a result of going to confession. I have long since ceased trying to measure this sort of progress in myself. I believe that we are incapable of doing so, that it would be bad for us if we could do so, and that all that matters is that our desire should be set upon God.

I suppose it is because of such doubts as these that many people are saying that we should pay more attention to the advice of the prayer book and reserve the sacrament of confession for those major sins about which our conscience cannot be quietened in any other way.

In this connection, I believe that people should always be treated as people, and not as coins to be fitted into a slot machine. Not long ago I had a man in my study who poured out to me the fairly horrific story of his life. I had no doubt that he was truly penitent and that God was forgiving him. Once I should have told him to go into the chapel and make his confession to me or to some other priest in the formal way, but now I gave him absolution where he was, and I cannot think that this was wrong.

A more radical criticism is that the sacrament of confession is too individualistic an exercise. It takes the penitent out of his social context. (We learn most things by seeing and hearing them done, and it would be helpful if we could learn how to confess, and how not to confess, by listening in, but this is something which we cannot do here!) The fact that corporate confession is not very meaningful for Anglicans—though we practise it often enough—suggests that we ought to take a deeper look at it. When we say, for instance, at the Eucharist, "We confess to God Almighty...", I tend to think, wrongly, that I am one of a bunch of individuals and when I say "we"

I mean "I". I could even be hoping that the churchwarden is confessing his recent outburst against the organist. If the thing is to be real, there must surely be some corporate self-examination first. Thus we could be led to confess together the selfishness of our affluent society, the fact that our congregation is a fellowship turned in upon itself, our share in the racial policies of South Africa, or our indifference to the break-up of family life in this land.

In church this might be difficult—so conservative are Anglicans here—unless perhaps the priest guided the thoughts of the congregation. But it could well be done in small groups. An increasing number of people find that their personal prayers—of every kind—become more meaningful when they are shared with others. It is probably a criticism of my too individualistic approach that I am not myself often helped in this way. Some of my friends tell me that they belong to a group in which there is such an atmosphere of trust that they can confess their individual sins to each other, but the fact that this practice was discredited both in the early church and in what used to be called the "Oxford" groups does not commend it to me, and I cannot see myself abandoning the sacramental way.

Corporate penitence is needed in all departments of our life, but perhaps nowhere so much as in our ecumenical activities.

Lord, I thank you for making me feel at home as the guest preacher in this Presbyterian church. The singing was good, the congregation reverent, the prayers scholarly and helpful.

Lord, I tried to express to them our penitence as Anglicans, not only for the grievous wrongs that English bishops have done in the past to the Church of Scotland, but also for our failure to show to them the episcopal office as it is rooted in the pastoral ideal of the gospel.

Lord, how easy it was to imply: I personally am all right, but I'm apologizing on behalf of other people

Apart from my share in the corporate wrongs—for we are all bound up together—help me, in this ecumenical context, to see and confess my own failures to love, my feelings of superiority, and my unwillingness to make sacrifices for unity.

The social aspect of confession has also to be remembered, for here reparation comes in. When I have quarrelled with another, unless I know that this was my fault—and it generally seems to be the other person's fault!—it is much easier to confess my sin to God than it is to apologize to the other person. If confession to God is just an easy way out, it means that my penitence is far from complete.

But to come back to sacramental confession, I should be sorry if I were thought to have said that it was outmoded. Rules can be deadening including the rule that you must go regularly to confession even when you know that you have already been forgiven, and so feel no need for forgiveness. Yet, if you are like me, unless you have rules your life will be spiritually disordered. The discipline of a periodical check-up, by means of a more detailed self-examination than I can achieve in my daily prayers, leads me to a deeper penitence, and so to a deeper understanding and appropriation of God's forgiveness. That is why, in spite of the dangers of legalism, I would always advise a regular use of sacramental confession.

The other thing that has to be done about our sins is to have a firm purpose of amendment. *A firm purpose*—those are the words that matter. God is not a taskmaster who is so hard that he looks for impossible results. He wants us to be perfect, but what he expects is that we should be aiming, with all the strength that he has given us, at that perfection.

Yet even if I do all these things, they are not of great significance. What ultimately matters is not my sins, but God's forgiveness; not my efforts, but Christ's sacrifice; not my selfishness, but God's love.

# 9

## ADORATION

In writing about the various aspects of prayer, I have not
been following any particular order, except perhaps to move
from the better known to the less known. Some would say
that I ought to have started with adoration, because it is—
though not many people believe this in materialistic
Johannesburg—the most important of all human activities.
De Chardin said, "The day is not far distant when humanity
will realize that biologically it is faced with a choice between
suicide and adoration." Von Hügel said, more simply, that
religion *is* adoration. I am aware that Von Hügel has no great
appeal for the present generation, and that his statement
raises many questions, not the least of which is, What is
religion? But it will do as a sign-post for the moment.

Many people feel nowadays that the love of our neighbour
comes first, and that we cannot begin to worship God until
we have learned how to do that. Perhaps I am rash in saying
that worship is our most important activity (though Jesus did
say that to love God is the "first" commandment) because
love of God and love of our neighbour must go along together
—just as a man cannot be said to be walking unless he has
one foot in the air and the other on the ground. As Cardinal
Suenens[1] puts it:

> We have to give a man bread *and* the sacred host. We
> have to teach the alphabet *and* the doctrine of Christ.
> We must offer them social security *and* the providence
> of God. We have to learn the value of work *and* the

[1] *Co-responsibility in the Church*, p. 56.

value of prayer. We have to save not only souls, but *men*.

Christ was the man for others precisely because he perpetually contemplated his Father and was always about his Father's business. If only I could be like that—which I know I am not—I should have solved the problem of living.

It took me a long time to understand what adoration meant, and I don't really understand it now, for we are talking about a mystery. Adoration is our reaction or response in the presence of God, and I should have to know God a great deal better than I do before my adoration could become what it ought to be. Yet I think that I have always known, without being able to analyse it, what adoration is, perhaps particularly as a child when wonder was more spontaneous in me than it has been in later years. The late twenties and the early thirties, which were my formative years, were a time of disillusionment and frustration, a time when I picked up a lot of cynicism, when I learned to be highly critical and suspicious of enthusiasm and of anything that gave easy answers. All this was destructive of the growth of adoration, and a good deal had to be unlearned before I could begin to go ahead again. For adoration arises from a feeling of surprise and wonder which we must not be afraid to express. But it becomes adoration only when that wonder is referred to God.

One year I had a few days off after Christmas and I spent them at Sequyane in Lesotho.

> Lord, thank you for this marvellous place. I am thrilled by the beauty of the green mountains, range upon range of them, with vast tracts of blue sky above; by the long shadows in the early morning and evening; by the trees and birds beside the river; by the maize and wheat growing in sheltered places; by the blue smoke rising from clustered rondavels; by the horsemen riding up steep bridle paths, and their greeting of *khotso*—peace—which seems to reflect the peace of heart that I find here.

> Lord, I read in the gospel today that your name is
> Immanuel, and you are certainly with us in this lovely
> and restful world.

An agnostic might well be equally moved by the beauty of
a scene like this, but I don't see how you can talk about
adoration in such a place unless you are aware of the presence
of God there. I take no credit at all for being aware of it—
it is something that God himself has shown me—but it seemed
natural there to turn to words from the psalms. "Sing unto
the Lord with thanksgiving ... who covereth the heaven with
clouds, and prepareth rain for the earth, and maketh the grass
to grow upon the mountains." The heavens declared the glory
of God—to me, though of course they declare something else
again to an atheist.

That day I had, however inadequately, a spirit of adoration. You will note that I wasn't in church at the time, though
I was worshipping God. Perhaps most of the things that cause
us surprise and wonder meet us when we are outside church,
and it is when we are inside that we can most easily *express*
our worship. For example, I was one day visiting a hospital
for child victims of polio. Some of them were terribly handicapped and deformed, but their courage and cheerfulness were
amazing—it was something out of this world—and I could
not help adoring God who had given them such gifts.

On another day I was admitted, after strict screening, into
the antiseptic atmosphere of the atomic reactor at Pelindaba.

> Lord, I could understand nothing, but nothing, about this
> reactor except that here was an immense power, an
> energy, which could be either lethal or beneficial.

> Lord, I wondered what all this had to do with worship in
> the local parish church, and how the altar and the
> reactor are correlated. The dedicated and youthful
> high priest who showed us round said that there are no
> atheists here, but he gave me the impression that he
> thought the altar—which I believe to be also the

centre of an immense power and energy—was about as incomprehensible to him as the reactor was to me.

Lord, it was frightening, awe-inspiring, to look at this comparatively small object, and to know how much power there was in it. But I believe that all creative power comes from you, and it was you that I was adoring there by the reactor.

Of course, this feeling of wonder does come to me in church also. Many people say that they have been aware of a certain religious building as being a holy place. "It is so easy to pray in that place—it has an atmosphere." For myself, I think of the roof-top chapel at Cowley, dark, silent, and vibrant with prayer. And sometimes God surprises us in the middle of dull or tiresome problems, because God is in our problems and difficulties always. If only I can look at him and adore him in those crises, I find, incidentally, that my problems are well on the way to being solved by him. What is hard is to remember him at once, instead of waiting until I have first used up my human resources, and then turning to him in desperation.

I suppose that there are some people who never feel surprise or wonder at anything. A young man once asked wistfully: "Can LSD be used legitimately when wonder has gone?" It is immensely sad when there is nothing that can lift up the heart, though I can appreciate the fact that the things which seem wonderful to me may not seem wonderful to others. When I got back from Lesotho I was talking to a friend about my holiday, and he said, "I can't think why you want to go to a place like that. There isn't even a bioscope in those mountains. If I were having a holiday, I should go to Durban." No doubt he finds an even greater number of things to cause him surprise and wonder in Durban.

I find air travel ordinary, and indeed boring, though I remember how much it used to frighten me twenty years ago. Today there was really nothing of interest except the man who made a fuss because the seat in which he sits four times a week was occupied by someone else, and the couple who demanded drinks just as the lights came up for "maak gordels vas". Then, at Bloemfontein, a young man came into the seat next to mine, and I discovered that he had never been in a plane before. His eyes were literally shining with excitement, and he was far nearer to a spirit of adoration than I was.

There are many different ways in which we can express our wonder once we have experienced it. We can say the first words that occur to us. They may sound fatuous, but they are at least a spontaneous expression of wonder—words like smashing, fab, just look at that, o-o-oh, isn't it marvellous?

We may lower our voices and whisper. This reaction is common in the historic cathedrals of Europe or, if it comes to that, in the Pretoria Monument. Or we may be altogether silent, lost, struck dumb, by the amazing thing that we have seen. Silent prayer—really being silent, as distinct from not saying words out loud—is an essential element in our spiritual life, and I shall have more to say about that in the next chapter.

When the wise men adored the Christ child at Bethlehem, they don't seem to have said anything. They simply presented their gifts. To give myself to God, as an expression of my wonder in his presence, is also an act of adoration and worship. This is *doing* the adoration. But how hard that is, and how easy to snatch back for myself the gift that I have just handed over!

I envy the people who can express their wonder in painting or poetry or music, but I sometimes find that I can use the works of artists in this way. If I am going to employ words to express my adoration, I always go back to the Bible for them. The classic example comes from the heavenly worship: Holy, holy, holy, is the Lord of Hosts. But here are a few from the many instances that I find satisfying:

Hallowed be thy name.

The Lord is in his holy temple; let all the earth keep silence before him.

Blessed be the name of the Lord; from this time forth for evermore.

O magnify the Lord our God ... for the Lord our God is holy.

> O the depth of the riches both of the wisdom and the knowledge of God! How unsearchable are his judgments, and his ways past finding out!
>
> Worthy art thou, O Lord and God, to receive glory and honour and power; for thou didst create all things; and by thy will they existed and were created.

Then there are liturgical—as distinct from biblical—sources which I occasionally like to use in my personal prayers. Such are the concluding words from the Gloria: "Thou only art holy; thou only art the Lord; thou only, O Christ, with the Holy Ghost art most high in the glory of God the Father." Or the collect endings, such as: "To thee, O Christ, with the Father and the Holy Spirit, be all honour and glory, world without end." And there are hymns, such as "Immortal, invisible" or "Let all mortal flesh keep silence".

Such private use of liturgical phrases is meaningful for me because it spills over from the public worship of the Church, and there, in the fellowship, I find a far more satisfying way of expressing the adoration that I feel—something far deeper than the oohs and the ahs of my own invention. But nothing is good enough for God, who is to be adored and worshipped for ever.

# 10

## CONTEMPLATION

There is a sort of prayer which includes all the ways of praying that I have so far mentioned. It is sometimes called meditation, which sounds rather alarming until we realize that in fact we do a lot of meditating every day. We meditate on what we shall wear, in what order we shall do our work, what we shall choose from the menu—if we are fortunate enough to have any choice in these matters. When applied to prayer it means choosing a theme and thinking it over, and then praying it over, using in as balanced a way as possible the different aspects of prayer, such as adoration, penitence, and the rest.

When I was preparing for ordination it was impressed upon me that meditation was an essential part of the life of a priest. I was told that priests who do not meditate become disillusioned and lethargic. I was told that half an hour a day was the least that I could spend on it, though obviously most lay people could not be expected to do as much as that.

The Church in its wisdom has never made any rule about it, even for priests. It has been said that the difference between an Anglican priest who neglects to say his office (an obligation which is imposed upon him by his prayer-book) and one who neglects his meditation is the same sort of difference as that between a man who fails to provide his wife with an adequate housekeeping allowance (a failure in obligation) and a man who forgets his wife's birthday (a failure in love).

I accepted all this in theory, but for the first six or seven years of my ministry I was far from regular about meditation. I made the excuse that, in the busy life of a London priest, there was not enough time. If I had been working late at night I couldn't get up early enough, and if I didn't do my meditation before breakfast there was no other convenient time. That was nonsense, because we can always find time to do the things that we really want to do. I expect a deeper reason was that I tried it, found it often difficult and dry, and then abandoned it in despair, except for the occasional days when I felt in the mood. I don't know why I supposed that prayer should always be easy or productive of joyful feelings, but that must have been my view at the time.

I might have gone on indefinitely like this, "fooling around", as Neville Ward puts it, "on the borders of sanctity". Not that there is much sanctity about me, either then or now; I was in fact fooling around on the borders of a disciplined prayer life. But I was helped by two things which seemed anything but divine interventions at the time, though looking back I can see the hand of God in them. One was the blitz. With bombs falling unpleasantly close, and my church a total wreck, I was forced to consider what the priorities were. The other was my desire to become a priest associate of the Society of St John the Evangelist, and Father O'Brien's refusal to admit me until I had proved that I could keep the rule of life. I accepted this as a challenge, for I had supposed that they would have been glad to have what I considered to be a man of my distinction on my own terms.

So I came gradually to understand that meditation is not an outpouring of feelings or a concern with my own needs and sins, but a turning to God. An illustration which has helped me is one that the Lord uses in the gospel, of the porter whose job is just to wait and listen for the bell. For most of the time he will do nothing but wait but, if he does this faithfully, he will be ready when his master has something to say to him.

Although in terms of minutes per day I have now for many years kept my appointed time for meditation, I would not wish to give the impression that I find it easy to be "on call". Since I am so often unrecollected during the rest of the day, it is hardly surprising that I should be plagued by distractions during my prayer-time also.

There are two ways that I have found of dealing with distractions. When my thoughts wander off to little things not connected with my prayers—what I shall do for lunch or whether I should make a certain phone call or why that server has such an astonishing hair style—I simply try to bring my attention back quietly to the matter in hand. St Teresa says that it is like flicking away flies that tickle your face when you are reading a book. It is important to do this gently, because to get angry with the flies does not help at all.

But sometimes the distractions are more serious, and then they are like, not flies, but a telephone calling you from your book to tell you of the serious illness of a friend. When a distraction of that sort occurs in my meditation—something which concerns a personal relationship, for instance, or a sphere of involvement to which I had not previously given much attention—I then switch off on to this new topic. It is here that I have found great profit in being able to meditate with a good conscience on the life-themes commended by the new spirituality.

It took me long to realize that there are no rules about the right way to meditate. Learned men have indeed laid down rules, some of which are as complicated as tracing a cross-country journey in a railway time-table. In my early days I found a certain fascination in trying out these methods in turn, but prayer seemed to get lost in the science of prayer. I was dissatisfied if the exercise was not completed according to the book of rules, and in the end I became so frustrated that I even began to compile my own rules.

It was a relief when I realized that all that was needed was a point at which to start—a short passage from one of the gospels, unless there is something else obviously to hand—and two or three set prayers at the beginning and the end, where these are found to be helpful. When I first took meditation seriously I used to read the passage slowly, ask what God was saying *to me* through the words, and then start speaking to him in as natural a way as I could, for meditation is personal communication with God. It might have gone something like this if I had been considering the healing of the paralytic.[1]

> Jesus, you were busy preaching and teaching in that house. Then there was an interruption, and this sick man was let down from the roof in front of you. You were not annoyed by the interruption. You *saw* him, and you saw him as a person who was in bad trouble. So you immediately stopped what you were doing, welcomed him, showed interest in him, listened to his problem, spoke to him and helped him.

> Jesus, I thank you that this is what you are always doing for me, especially when I came to you in that trouble over disloyalty yesterday.

> Jesus, I think what you are saying to me in all this is that, when someone in trouble comes to me, I must not be annoyed by the interruption—as I was when that ordinand came (and I am sorry about that)—but I must welcome him, and go out of my way to help him.

> Jesus, I don't want to leave all this in the air, so I promise you that at least the first interruption of today will find me ready to do what you did at Capernaum.

As the years went on, the pattern changed somewhat. Less time was spent on considering the meaning of the passage, and I found myself content with what are called "acts of prayer", perhaps often repeated—acts of love, penitence, resignation, gratitude, desire, adoration, or short aspirations such as: "My God and my all!" or "My God, I hope in you, I believe in you, I love you". In other words, the imagination and the mind were becoming less important in prayer than the will and the affections.

Abbot Butler[2] suggests that it is normal for every praying Christian to pass through a crisis, analogous to the crisis of

[1]Mark 2.1ff.
[2]In the appendix to *Prayer, an adventure in living*.

72

adolescence, whereby formal and sensible prayer (which means prayer in which thoughts and feelings are predominant) passes into a prayer which seems cold and dead, and yet which is more deeply real than anything which has preceded it.

This does not seem to be true in my own case. Once I had moved out of a spasmodic and irregular practice of prayer, there have been developments, such as the increasing use of "acts". But at every stage it has been interesting and, although there has been a great deal of deadness and coldness, this has been mainly my own fault. Various things have kept my interest alive—the eschatological context of the war years, the baroque atmosphere of my first mission station, a period of "prayerful ponderings" which issued in written notes, and now the new spirituality.

> Lord, does this mean that I am still in the adolescent stage of prayer, or that I am incapable of advanced prayer, or that the crisis is still ahead of me?

> Lord, whatever the explanation is, keep me humble about my prayer, and let me pray in whatever way you want me to pray; and above all, let me go on praying.

I suppose the reason why I find it difficult to analyse any development in my prayer life is that there is a continual ebb and flow. It is not that last month my prayer consisted mainly of intellectual considerations and formulated sentences, whereas this month it has moved on to something different. It is rather that sometimes one form predominates and sometimes another, and it is only by looking back over the years that I can see, on balance, some change of direction.

Another thing that I have come to value increasingly is silence, though this is more often in desire than in achievement.

> Lord, I want to be silent, in order to enter into your presence and hear what you are saying. I want to be still and know that you are God (Ps. 46.10).

> Lord, I want to be silent because I know that I am already in your presence.

73

Lord, I want to be silent as you, the suffering servant, were silent in your passion.

Lord, I want to be silent physically (but I am restless) and mentally (but I am distracted), and so let you construct for me an interior garden of Eden, a garden enclosed for prayer (Cant. 4.12).

Lord, I want to enter into prayer as a mystery rather than as a problem, to centre down to the still core of my being, and to rest in you there.

This brings me close to what I take to be the meaning of contemplation. Until a generation ago, contemplation was generally regarded as the preserve of enclosed nuns and people with special gifts of prayer, although it is true that St Francis de Sales wrote about contemplation for ordinary people, and *The Cloud of Unknowing* was also written with such people in mind. It is now seen as the normal development of meditation, though this does not mean that those who find it are more holy or more "advanced" than those who pray in other ways.

But what is contemplation? It is a prayer which moves towards simplicity. Spoken words are gradually reduced to silence. That is why it is impossible to describe it, because it cannot be put into words. From what little I know of it I can say that it is a prayer of expectant silence, and yet it is also a restful thing, a simple, loving attention to God in himself. It has nothing to do with mystical experience, if by that is meant visions, trances, or ecstasies. It means knowing God rather than knowing about him.

It would be ridiculous for me to call myself a contemplative, because it is only for brief moments that my prayer takes this form. I am encouraged to read that even so great an authority as St Augustine found the same thing. He said that it was only in transitory experiences that he had had glimpses of "a place of rest where there would be the full enjoyment of the absolute and true God", a place where he could "breathe the clear air of serenity and eternity". He said that, if such experience were to reach fulfilment in him, "it would be something entirely different from my present life. But ... I am sucked back to my habits and I find myself held fast."

Those who are experts in contemplation say that it is an awareness, in the depths of the soul, of God's presence—a presence that is not confined to times of prayer—and a gladness at being there, a silent adoration and a peace in the presence. It is a state in which we have ceased to long for God, because we know that God possesses and controls the whole of our being, and our only desire is for a deeper communion with him.

But my name is not Augustine Baker and I can speak only of what I know. The moments of contemplation, however brief, that I have received, are deeply real to me, and there is a sense in which I feel that here I am most at home, most truly myself.

If I were to try to analyse one of my current meditation periods, I think it would go something like this. First I read in the gospel how Jesus came through closed doors into the frightened fellowship and gave them his peace. I pictured the scene with my imagination. Once I would have spent a long time over this, but today it went through like a movie flash. I then thought about it with my mind. Again this would once have taken a longer time still, and commentaries and versions would have been brought in to help. Even now I might have spent much time on this stage if I had been drawn to ponder a life-theme, such as a failure in our priestly fellowship owing to the lack of the Lord's loving presence. Next I talked to the Lord about what he had said to me through the incident. At first I had to make myself look at him and speak to him, so wrapped up in self was I, and I had to make myself tell him that I adored him who is the giver of peace and the lover who takes away fear, tell him that I knew I was receiving his peace into my being. After a while these aspirations became, though for a few moments only, as natural to me as breathing. There was no longer anything forced about it, my soul being centred upon him whom I know.

I think this means that I moved through mental prayer to

affective prayer, to contemplation. If I were a real contemplative I suppose I should go straight to contemplation and stay there. I don't know if the experts would approve of this— perhaps I ought to care more for their opinion—but it seems to me that the great thing is not to understand what is happening so much as to pray.

I believe that contemplation is a possibility for everyone who has a sincere desire to pray and who is prepared to follow the path that begins with meditation. For those with a simple faith, it is probably easier than for those who know what doubt means and who are perplexed by the problems of prayer. But it can be learned by all and, as the 1968 Lambeth Report says,[1] we need to "learn to keep still and listen to God. This means fostering each man's capacity for contemplation."

If this form of prayer comes more naturally to others than it does to me, that is something they should thank God for. To those who have never tried it I would suggest that they start now. To those who have been discouraged by its difficulties and given it up I would propose that they start again. We should never belittle our prayers, because they are not *our* prayers, but the prayers of the Spirit who prays within us. St Paul[2] understood our predicament well enough. He said that, though none of us really knows how to pray, even our inarticulate groanings are signs of the Holy Spirit's presence; and the Spirit cooperates with those who love God in teaching them how to pray.

[1] p. 76.
[2] Rom. 8.26–30.

# 11

## PUBLIC PRAYERS

So far I have been writing about private prayers, but much of what I have said applies also to my prayers in church. Some new problems arise here.

I asked a distinguished layman who had recently retired from a big administrative job in the city to examine the organization and structures of our diocese with a view to introducing some urgently needed improvements. His first reaction was to say that organization can never be an end in itself. If you want to organize a shoe-factory, for instance, you must know whether you plan to make quality shoes or mass-produced ones and whether your aim is to make as big a profit as possible or to provide a livelihood for handicapped people. So his first question was to ask, What is the Church for? And he was shocked to find that several clergy and laymen could give no clear answer. I suppose this was because many of us are so busy getting on with the job that we do not pause to ask what the job itself is.

> Lord, what is your Church *for*? It is your body—the expression of yourself—here on earth, so it should do what you did in Palestine and "greater things than these".

> Lord, I hear you saying that it is to be
> a worshipping Church
> and a serving Church
> and a healing Church
> and a Church on mission
> and a Church which is a fellowship.

Lord, all these things are necessary, but some parts of the
programme are seen as more urgent in one generation
than in another. Teach us to see where our priorities lie.
Teach us whether we are right to see them now in our
serving and mission work. Teach us to find a true
balance.

If I narrow down this general question and ask why I
encourage people to attend church services, I find myself
caught up in controversy. One of my friends is a teenager,
modern, mini-skirted, and attractive, not overstocked with
brains—but then you can't have everything, can you? Her
parents were delighted when she volunteered to go with them
to Easter communion, because she had not been at all regular
at church. When she got back, she was in a bad temper,
grumbled about the service, said that she could see no point
in it, and remarked that it would have been better to have
said her prayers at home.

Lord, I don't think that she had any doubts about you, or
she would not have talked about saying her prayers at
home. I thank you that she does believe in you, and I
ask you to increase her faith and understanding.

Lord, I think that she was protesting against the way in
which the service was taken, and I know that many
agree with her in her impatience with the familiar and
the predictable, the slovenly and the boring, the
parsonical voice, the priest who stands first on one leg
and then on the other.

Lord, forgive us when we resent such criticism as being
an attack on the Church that we love, for we know
that we are at fault, and deep down we desire to hear
in such criticism your deserved rebuke to us.

What goes much deeper than the way in which services are
taken is the tension between the old and the new, which is as
obvious in the field of church services as everywhere else. I
have thought about this in connection with private prayers,

but there it is easier to deal with, for only I need make the decision on how my prayers are to be said. In church I also have to consider the views of my neighbour.

In 1966 Carl Burke wrote a book called *God is for real, man*. It is an attempt to re-tell some Bible stories in the idiom of young people from an American gaol, and to show—as Bruce Kenrick says in the Foreword—"how much nearer the reality of the Bible is to everyday reality than it is to much of our 'Sundays-only' church life". Here, for instance, is his parable of the lost sheep:

> There was a used-car lot at the corner of Main and Fillmore. The owner had one hundred heaps on it. If one of the heaps was snitched, would the owner go and look for it? You bet he would. He would never give up looking till he found it.

> Suppose he found it at North and Main. What would he do? Well, he would "rev. it up, man", to see if it's OK. When he gets it back to the yard, he would show it to the gang to have it checked out. If it checks out OK they would all be happy, 'cause that one heap is just as important as the 99 that no one stole. Well, this is the way it will be when one guy goes straight. One guy is just as important to God as 99 are who have always been OK. This is for real—God is just as interested in you as the used-car lot owner is in his heap.

The book was banned by the South African censors. The publishers (it is a Collins "Fontana") were naturally distressed by the apparent slur on their reputation and they asked me to review it. I expected it to deal with race problems or politics or sex, but there was no more about these things than there is in the Bible itself. It simply was that its idiom was so radical that the censor thought that it was making fun of the Bible and so he banned it as being blasphemous. Fortunately he reconsidered his decision and the book may now be legally bought in this country.

What are we to do about the old-new tension in church services? I myself appreciate the stately English, the dignified cadences, the fixed forms and rules of the prayer-book, but I know that many others think that worship has thus become frozen in a seventeenth-century language and format. Some rejoice in experimentation and others are horrified at it.

It is not a matter of age, for some young people prefer the old ways and some old people the new. I sometimes wonder if my like of both old and new makes me look like an elderly roué seeking to preserve his youth.

Lord, help me neither to grasp at a thing just because it is new, nor to reject it just because it is new, but rather give me an open mind to weigh up objectively what is good and bad in the new, and so to see where you are in relation to it.

The tension goes, however, even deeper still, down to our basic belief about God. In an earlier chapter I said that many people nowadays find it hard to think of God as transcendent. The word "supernatural" seems to mean nothing to them. This world, the world of science and technology, of human aspirations and planning, is the only world of which they are aware. Even if transcendence is meaningful for them they cannot see how God can be both transcendent and immanent at the same time. If we are searching for God, it seems to them, we must either search along a horizontal line and look for him here and now in the world, in the love and the suffering around us; or we must look for him along a vertical line, in his eternity and his infinity and his separateness from the world. I wonder if it would be true to say that the "young" are mainly in favour of the horizontal line of service, and the "old" of the vertical line of faith?

These various tensions are all reflected in the answer we might give to my question, *Why* should I encourage anyone to attend a church service?

Lord, thank you—it was *a nice service,* so they all said.
The young like expressing themselves through guitars

and pop hymns, and sharing in the prayers and lessons. The old who were there felt with it for once, and they liked to see a great crowd of young people in church. It was informal, they enjoyed themselves, and they went home feeling good.

Lord, forgive me for my easy criticism of the liturgical shapelessness, the jejune hymns, the lack of adoration.

Yet, Lord, there was a reality about it and, because of this, many are being drawn to you through the sacraments. Perhaps I was judging by the standards of worship what was really a missionary get-together, with you in the chair. And surely that is something that you approve of!

Movements to make our services more relevant to everyday life, less complicated, and more open to congregational participation have a place in many Anglican churches; but some of our young people, impatient at not finding them in their own parish, are beginning to look for them in other churches. A young ordinand told me recently that he is being attracted to the Baptist church, with its tradition of free worship and spontaneous prayer, which he found refreshing and sincere compared with what goes on in his own parish church. I had to tell him that this was one of the main reasons why I left the Baptist church, in which I was brought up, because I found there that I was at the mercy of the individual minister, and that I was attracted by the objective and timeless worship of the Anglican church!

This leads us into the other side of the main tension, to those who favour the vertical line and who see a church service as something that is offered to the eternal, infinite God. There is a mystery to be adored, and it is felt that a service which is completely understandable robs us of that mystery. What is basic, according to this view, is not our feelings as we worship, but our being united with Christ's love for his Father. What is important is not the prayer of my insignificant self, but the prayers of the Church, in which I join. Even when we ourselves have no "hearty desire to pray", we are part of a praying community which has just that.

Those who look for a vertical line rejoice in the "help that comes from above", through sacramental grace and prayer and God's word, but they are aware of a danger here. It is possible to concentrate on what we want from God, rather than on what we, in union with Christ's sacrifice, can give to God. Because I am aware of this danger, I cannot agree with the divorced and remarried couple who said to me that, as they could no longer receive communion, there was no point in their coming to the Eucharist until such time as they could be restored.

There is, of course, no problem when our feelings lift us up spontaneously to God in church, but I am sure that this is not a common experience, nor does God mean it to be so.

> Lord, you have given me enormous joy and consolation through religion, as well as putting me through some crises, but there are not many times when I sensibly feel your presence. I remember so well one of the first of these. As an undergraduate, soon after my conversion to the Anglican faith, at a church in the east end of London, early on a dark, foggy, weekday morning, there was a Eucharist with about a dozen people present, and after my communion I felt as if I was walking on air.

> Lord, I thank you for that, and for a few parallel occasions. I know that I was not worthy of them, and it was probably because my faith was so weak that I needed them. I think also that they have mostly come, as this one certainly did, when I was involved with the underprivileged.

> Lord, as I kneel before the altar today, whatever may be the present state of my feelings, I do at least know what adoration is, and I know also that greater love for my neighbours would help to make it more real.

But feelings cannot be depended upon as a basis for our Christian life. In my younger days obligation was a word that was much used. We should worship God because it is our duty to do so. This is unpopular doctrine in the permissive society yet for myself I must have some means of fixing my will on God when I feel emotionally dead, or only just very tired.

I once received a letter from a schoolmaster, aged about thirty, in which he said: "I used to enjoy going to the Eucharist on weekdays as well as on Sundays, and reading the Bible and other religious books, and I felt the presence of God in me as I prayed. But now I find a change in my spiritual life. I still pray mornings and evenings and on Sundays, but I don't feel the presence of God in me any more. When I pray, I don't seem to notice what I am saying, when I go to confession it is hard to know what to confess, and I go to communion because it is a habit, though I don't feel the urgency of it any more. I am very worried about this. Please, Father, tell me what I am doing wrong."

> Lord, I told him to thank you for teaching him to pray objectively. At the beginning of his spiritual life he had to be given consolations, like a child being encouraged with sweets to do something hard. But now he was growing up, and learning to love you for your own sake.

> Lord, that was twenty years ago. Was I right? For myself, I know I was right, since this attitude has been a sure anchor for me during stormy times.

> Lord, I think that, if I was answering a modern enquirer, I should first have to offer him the new resources that you have given us—new translations of Bible and prayer-book, new lectionaries, new provisions for the use of the psalter, and contemporary forms of prayer.

> Lord, I thank you for these new resources. Help me to use them better, and yet not to think that I have "done wrong" when it comes to just going on and on.

In addition to these new resources, we need much more Bible study in order to bring to life the resources that we already have in our church services. Even the most ardent supporters of the vertical line must admit that, since it is we who are praising God, what we say must come from our hearts if it is to be real.

> Lord, what a revolutionary song is this Magnificat which your Mother sang! It is honestly surprising that the Church of the Province of South Africa, which uses it so often, has not been prosecuted for this under the Prevention of Communism Act. The fact that we haven't been means that the government knows that we don't believe what we say.

> Lord, you are the mighty one, and those who set themselves up as mighty are usurping your place; so that you must throw them out; and, in scattering the proud, you turn the world upside down. You exalt only the humble, you give food only to the hungry and—most shocking of all to us in northern Johannesburg—you send away the rich!

> Lord, I desire—or, at least, I desire to desire—the humility and the hunger and the poverty of the Beatitudes and the Magnificat, so that I may be exalted into your presence.

I have been speaking as if we have to make a choice between the horizontal and the vertical lines. But in fact we need them both. I find the point of intersection here and now in the Eucharist and, further back, in the cross.

> Lord, here at the foot of the cross I see the great vertical line that runs from earth into the transcendental, and that proclaims both your finality and our responsibility before you, and I adore you there.

> Lord, as I look up at the cross, I see your arms stretched out in the horizontal line that runs through society, through our neighbours, through sufferers, and through believers, and I pledge myself to your service.

> Lord, where the two lines are perfectly joined, there is

the total cross. Where the powers are trying to keep them apart, but where they just touch as if accidentally, there must be an explosion.

Lord, I adore you and I commit myself to you, the one Christ, in the totality of the cross, and I accept your total salvation.

What is a church service for? Ideally it should be for all these purposes that I have mentioned—for the adoration of God in his glory, a means of grace, an expression of our Christian fellowship, and a way of drawing others to him. With such tremendous aims, it is hardly surprising that I rarely feel satisfied with any church service that I attend.

As I am sometimes depressed by the inadequacy of my personal prayers, so I am depressed by the inadequacy of our public prayers. Church services ought to inspire me and uplift me from this world of space and time, and yet give me the strength to live in this world of space and time. They ought to attract the non-Christian to the fellowship of the Church and to the worship of God. I thank God that they sometimes do all this, but all too often they fail to do so.

It is wrong of me to be depressed or to grumble about these failures. Even if I were able to produce and to conduct a service which seemed perfect to those taking part in it, it would certainly not seem perfect to another generation. We have to use the resources that we have and to be continually on the look out for new resources, remembering that God never stands still.

And as for the tension between transcendence and immanence, I know that I have to try to live within it and to express this twofold belief through our church services in the best way that can be devised. This is a task for which we need the dynamic help of everyone to whom prayer is real.

# 12

## SOME PRAYERS FROM MY NOTEBOOK

### I. ASH WEDNESDAY

In many of our churches we keep the ancient custom on this day of blessing ashes, which are made from the palm crosses of the previous year. The congregation come to kneel at the altar-rail, and the priest, dipping his thumb in the ashes, makes the sign of the cross on the forehead of each one, saying, "Remember, O man, that dust thou art and unto dust thou shalt return".

Lord, today I noticed particularly an elderly woman who looked so ill that she might have turned to dust at any moment. But I also noticed a very beautiful girl and several healthy, eager children, and I felt a quite Greek sense of the sadness of mortality when I thought of *them* turning to dust.

Then, Lord, I wondered about the meaning of the words. They are true of the body—in so far as we can make a separation between body and soul—but are they true of the "man"?

Lord, I believe that we all come from you, and that unto you we shall return. Our end will be, not dust, but resurrection. Nothing that is beautiful and good will be lost in this process, and we should be so living the resurrection life now that the physical process of death has little importance for us.

## 2. BEGGARS

Wherever I went in the Lesotho mountains, grown people and children alike held out their hands for cents or sweets. "Happy Christmas" was a standard greeting, meaning "Give me a Christmas box". The Europeans said, "The begging here is terrible"; and my friend, a most generous person, would give biscuits to none but two angelic little girls who did not beg, and who retired into a bush to eat them before the older children saw what was happening.

Lord, I know that there is a danger of pauperization, and in the past this has been carried to excess by missionaries in your name. But is it not a privilege for us to be able to give to those who have so little?

And, Lord, do you not tell us to ask, and to go on asking, until we receive?

Lord, these people know well enough how to give to each other when they are in need. Is there anything wrong in them teaching us how to give?

## 3. I CORINTHIANS 13

If every day I celebrate the Holy Eucharist, and every Sunday preach converting sermons, but speak without love, I am simply a gong booming.

If I am up to date with radical theology, and know how the Church should be renewed, and have enough faith to change its structures, but am without love, then I am nothing at all.

If I could lay hands on all the Church's endowments and give them, with my own savings, to Inter-church Aid, and if I took part in protest movements that led to my own removal, but am without love, it will do me no good whatever.

Lord, I want to love you with all my heart, all my understanding, and all my strength and to love my neighbour as myself.

## 4. FAMILY DAY

Lord, the words and the action of Judas—"Master, master" and the kiss—were fine, and this is what I say and do every morning at the Eucharist. Forgive me that other words and other actions often follow which are not consistent with these. Above all forgive me if I ever use these words and this action with deliberate hypocrisy.

Lord, forgive our country which is involved in just this sort of hypocrisy today. Forgive *us,* for we cannot stand over against our country, as if we did not share in its faults. Forgive us that we have a public holiday for Family Day and then—

> make it illegal for a husband and wife to sleep together in certain places;

> call the wives and children of the urban African labourer "superfluous appendages";

> support the migratory labour system, which has been called "a raging cancer in the lives of the Bantu population";

> stop two young people, who are deeply in love, from marrying because it is found at the last moment that the colour of one of them is in doubt.

Lord, renew a right spirit within us, so that we may please you when we say "Master, master", and kiss you.

## 5. NEW BUILDINGS

They are tearing down yet another building in the next block to us and the noise of the pneumatic drills, the falling masonry, and the coming and going of heavy lorries is terrible. But eventually they will get rid of the rubbish, and on the same rock they will build up something more useful and beautiful than the present structure.

Lord, you too were torn to pieces. They did that to you in your ministry when you were attacked, and the crowds

88

left you, and all the beauty that you had built up was pulled down. They did it to you especially on the cross where you were utterly destroyed, with a maximum of pain and noise, and tumbled into a tomb. Yet out of the rock which is you came your risen life in all its glory.

Lord, if you are going to tear me to pieces, I beg your help that I may put up willingly with a lot of noise and pain, and that I may accept the fact that the stand on which my life is built may be useless and unproductive for a time, until the new building is up.

Lord, help me to understand that all the difficulties and hurts and frustrations of life are part of your plan to tear down my self, so that you can build me into a new person.

## 6. FRIENDS

Lord, this coloured head-waiter served me at the hotel table, as I had served him earlier that morning at your table in the location church. We were friends of each other because we were your friends.

So, Lord, when I first saw him in the dining-room, it seemed natural to me to shake him by the hand. But then I wondered whether I would have done that had he been white. Was I being condescending to him, being a racist? I also wondered whether my action had embarrassed him in the eyes of the other guests, by suggesting to them that he was endeavouring to live above his "station in life".

Lord, these race relationships are very complicated in practice, but I believe that you want your friends to err—if it is an error—on the side of showing their friendliness, however many eyebrows may be raised by this.

## 7. LORD OF THE NOT YET

Jesus, you are lord of the here and now, of the village

green and the stock exchange, of the love-in and the Saigon inferno, of the coffee-bar and the moon landing, of the special branch and the sensitivity course, of the fashionable dinner-party and the white hoboes, of the beer-hall and the Berlin wall, of all our thoughts and feelings and decisions this day.

Jesus, you are also the lord of the not yet, of the generations which shall be born, of the glory which we shall see in paradise, of the cosmos when this world shall be no more, of the day of judgment and of your coming in power.

Jesus, help me always to remember the not yet in the here and now.

## 8. GROUP AREAS

The black areas continue to be moved further away from town, and in each of them a new church has to be built. The compensation received for the old one supplies only a fraction of the cost of this, the people themselves cannot pay for the new building, and the white Christians are often reluctant to help.

Lord, that is how I see it—you want me to provide them with a place to worship in and a pastor to live among them—and I know that I am seeing only a pitiably small part of the real problem.

Lord, I do not know what it feels like to live in a group area. I know that the people have to get up early and travel in crowded trains and buses to their work. I know that the streets are not safe to walk about in at night. I know that they complain above all things about the inadequacies of Bantu education. I know that a whole lot of people, coming from different places and suddenly thrown together, cannot form a community overnight.

Lord, I know all these things and much more, but I don't

know what it feels like to live in a group area, and I
am not permitted to find this out for myself. I should
have expected an atmosphere of hatred, but I thank you
that there is much compassion, much understanding,
much laughter, even though that is often only a paper-
ing over of the cracks.

Lord, help the white people of this land to see this as a
human problem and—even if policies cannot be changed
—to treat these people as people made in your image.

### 9. CHRISTIAN AND JEW

Lord, I thank you for this Jewish doctor whom I met at a
party last night. I thank you for his humility and compassion and for his profound concern about things that
matter. He is searching for the way of conscience through
our political situation, and he cares in practice for
under-privileged Africans.

Lord, I found myself much more in sympathy with him
than with the charming but nominal churchmen who
formed the rest of the party.

Lord, you said to Mary Magdalene, "Touch me not." Why
is it that I am allowed to touch you, and this doctor is
not—at least in any sacramental or credal sense? Are
you telling me again that creeds and sacraments do not
matter as much as I think that they do? That love and
integrity are the first things?

### 10. WHY DON'T THEY COME IN?

Michel Quoist speaks of the strangers who pour into his
house and overwhelm him, and I too have had some experience
of this.

Yet sometimes, Lord, I open the door and stand there
ready to welcome others in, but they hurry by, perhaps
with a friendly smile or perhaps without noticing me.

There is this schoolboy, Lord, who has no more than

monosyllables for me, and who seems relieved when the time has come for him to leave.

There was the man at the party, Lord, who, just as we seemed to have got started on something, broke off in the middle of a sentence because he had seen someone whom he really wanted to talk to.

There was the fat man in the plane, Lord, who looked friendly, but he could not step over the threshold.

There is that priest, Lord, and I never know whether he is in or out. He certainly makes few demands upon me.

Why is it, Lord? Perhaps it is because I am blocking the doorway and, if my horrid self could get out of the way, these people would be able to come in—*you* would be able to come in.


## 11. ETHNIC GROUPING

The Bantu Affairs Department increasingly insists on ethnic groupings in the big locations. They say this helps to preserve all that is best in tribal culture, and that it makes for better education, because each school has only one language as the medium of instruction. Its effect, however, is to make Africans more divided, and even ethnic churches are now being asked for.

Lord, the more closely we look, the more walls we see that have been built by human possessiveness. Forgive us, Lord, especially for the walls that we are building inside your church.

Lord, some Africans are saying that you too are in favour of ethnic grouping, because at first you refused to help the Syrophoenician woman (Mark 7.25f). Whatever your reason was for doing that, you must have been pleased with the way she dealt with a segregated situation—by humility and hope and refusing to give up. Grant us grace to do the same.

## 12. THE ARTIST

This artist showed me over her studio and explained how some of her inspirations had come to her. She had, for instance, a piece of bark, shaped like a human figure, which had led her to paint a crucifixion, with the women portrayed as hollow figures, emptied of all feeling and hope.

Lord, you showed me through her how all natural objects are either whorls spiralling up to you, or radiations reminding us of the sun of righteousness.

Lord, I thank you for teaching me in this way. Open my eyes wider, so that I may see more of the wonderful things of your creation and your law and your salvation.

## 13. TOP PEOPLE

I spent an hour and a half answering the questions of a lecturer from Rhodes University in connection with a survey project into the "élite"—the one thousand top people of South Africa. They wanted to know how we reached our present position, what are our views on current problems, and how we see the future of this country.

Lord, I was flattered at being chosen as one of the élite, but I had to make a protest and say that this was scarcely a Christian way of looking at life—to assess a man by his status, his ambition, his way of life, or his standard of living.

Lord, you are among us as one who serves; and if I am to be allowed into your presence at all it must be only as a servant, as one who hangs around until you give him a job to do.

Yet, Lord, I wonder how sincere my protest really was, because I went on answering the questions, and I haven't any serious intention of voluntarily altering my way of life.

Teach me, good Lord, to serve you as you deserve to be served.

Provided that he has the proper papers and the promise of a job, provided that he comes alone and for a time only, this African may enter the urban area.

Jesus, you had to face influx control at Bethlehem. They must have been kind to you, for you had no papers at all and your job seemed mythical. But they made it plain that you came on your own, and that you would not be allowed to stay here for long.

Jesus, you have to face influx control at the gate of my heart. The decision is mine (I think) not yours, as to whether you are allowed in. If you do enter, remember that some of the areas are white and so not for you. And understand that you must come alone, without any of those relatives of yours. And you will have to go when I tell you to.

Jesus, come in—force your way in if necessary—and ocupy all the areas of my life, and bring with you anyone you like, and stay for always.

## 15. ROOM FOR ALL

Lord, as many as touched you were made whole. But first they had to want to touch you, and it is clear that they did want this, for they ran to you and besought you before they touched you (Mark 6.53ff).

Lord, in this nativity play, where you were represented as the child of a Soweto mother, visited by magi from Lesotho, Swaziland, and Botswana, people gathered to adore you, for there was room for all—Anglicans too, Europeans too, Zionists too, tsotsis too, the whole audience too.

Lord, this was all very moving, and I am sure that it is true. But we do not live this way. If other denominations want to touch you they had better become Anglicans, or at least enter into serious dialogue with us. If the independent countries want to advance they had better make an alliance with South Africa. As for the Zionists, it is hard to take them seriously. The tsotsis —well only the specialist has a vocation to draw *them* in. Everybody?—that is impossible.

Lord, you know who wants to touch you; you welcome them all. Give us the openness of your love.

### POSTSCRIPT

Jesus, because this has become a devotional moment in my prayer, do not let me fall into the pietism that is so prevalent all round me, and so forget the people in Johannesburg who are actually being "effluxed" at this moment. They are some of the people that you bring in with you to my heart. Show me how to help them, or at least to be sympathetic with them, Lord.